# studysync®

## Reading & Writing Companion

# Taking a Stand

studysync

studysync.com



Send all inquiries to:
BookheadEd Learning, LLC
610 Daniel Young Drive
Sonoma, CA 95476

8 QSX 22 B

Cover, ©iStock.com/prudkov, ©iStock.com, ©iStock.com/alexey_boldin, ©iStock.com/skegbydave

# STUDENT GUIDE

## GETTING STARTED

Welcome to the StudySync Reading and Writing Companion! In this booklet, you will find a collection of readings based on the theme of the unit you are studying. As you work through the readings, you will be asked to answer questions and perform a variety of tasks designed to help you closely analyze and understand each text selection. Read on for an explanation of each section of this booklet.

# CORE ELA TEXTS

In each Core ELA Unit you will read texts and text excerpts that share a common theme, despite their different genres, time periods, and authors. Each reading encourages a closer look with questions and a short writing assignment.

## INTRODUCTION

An Introduction to each text provides historical context for your reading as well as information about the author. You will also learn about the genre of the excerpt and the year in which it was written.

## FIRST READ

During your first reading of each excerpt, you should just try to get a general idea of the content and message of the reading. Don't worry if there are parts you don't understand or words that are unfamiliar to you. You'll have an opportunity later to dive deeper into the text.

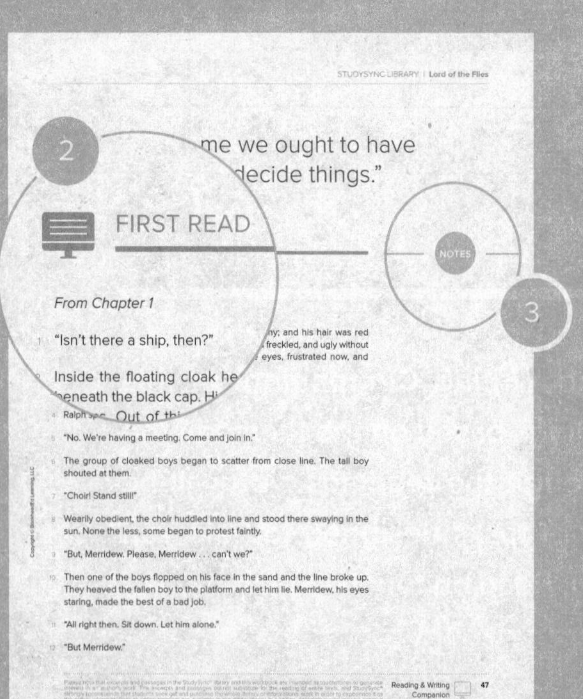

## NOTES

Many times, while working through the activities after each text, you will be asked to **annotate** or **make annotations** about what you are reading. This means that you should highlight or underline words in the text and use the "Notes" column to make comments or jot down any questions you may have. You may also want to note any unfamiliar vocabulary words here.

## 4 THINK QUESTIONS

These questions will ask you to start thinking critically about the text, asking specific questions about its purpose, and making connections to your prior knowledge and reading experiences. To answer these questions, you should go back to the text and draw upon specific evidence that you find there to support your responses. You will also begin to explore some of the more challenging vocabulary words used in the excerpt.

## 5 CLOSE READ & FOCUS QUESTIONS

After you have completed the First Read, you will then be asked to go back and read the excerpt more closely and critically. Before you begin your Close Read, you should read through the Focus Questions to get an idea of the concepts you will want to focus on during your second reading. You should work through the Focus Questions by making annotations, highlighting important concepts, and writing notes or questions in the "Notes" column. Depending on instructions from your teacher, you may need to respond online or use a separate piece of paper to start expanding on your thoughts and ideas.

## 6 WRITING PROMPT

Your study of each excerpt or selection will end with a writing assignment. To complete this assignment, you should use your notes, annotations, and answers to both the Think and Focus Questions. Be sure to read the prompt carefully and address each part of it in your writing assignment.

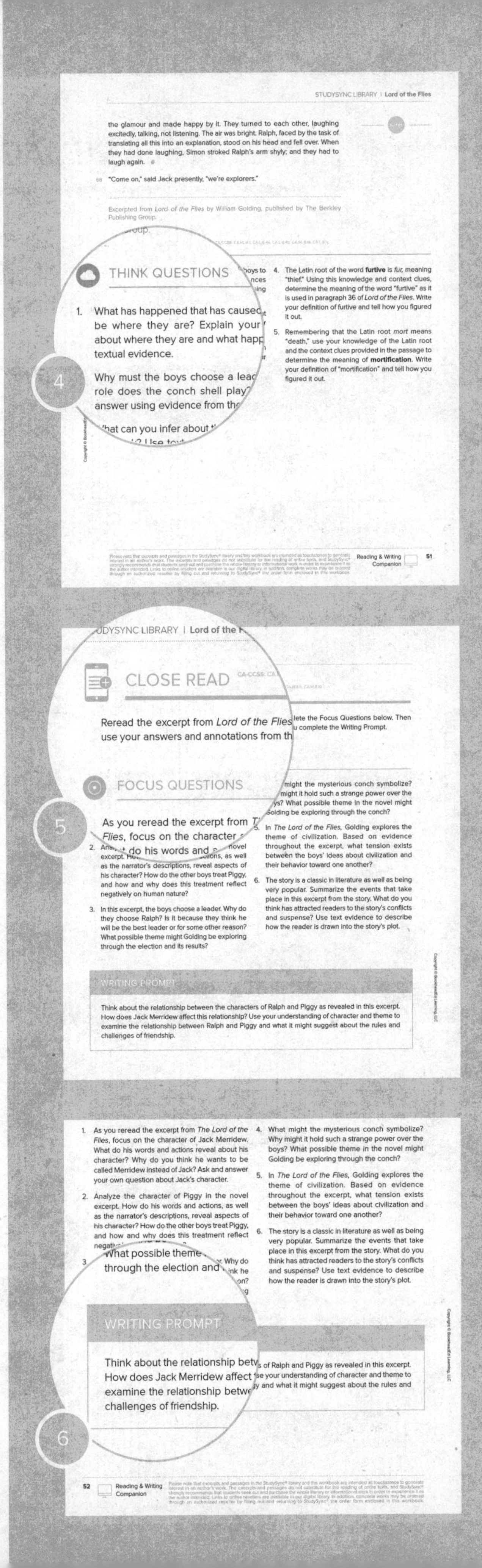

# ENGLISH LANGUAGE DEVELOPMENT TEXTS

The English Language Development texts and activities take a closer look at the language choices that authors make to communicate their ideas. Individual and group activities will help develop your understanding of each text.

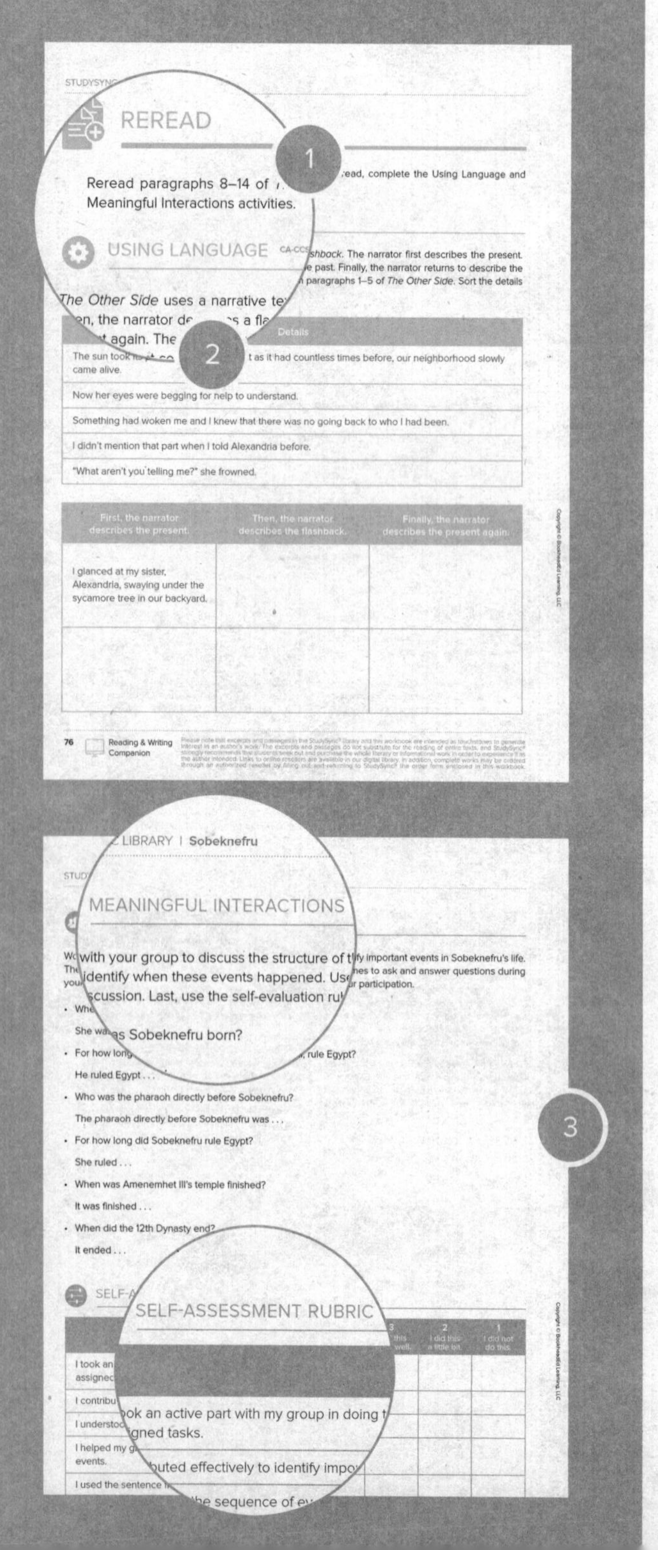

## REREAD

After you have completed the First Read, you will have two additional opportunities to revisit portions of the excerpt more closely. The directions for each reread will specify which paragraphs or sections you should focus on.

## USING LANGUAGE

These questions will ask you to analyze the author's use of language and conventions in the text. You may be asked to write in sentence frames, fill in a chart, or you may simply choose between multiple-choice options. To answer these questions, you should read the exercise carefully and go back in the text as necessary to accurately complete the activity.

## MEANINGFUL INTERACTIONS & SELF-ASSESSMENT RUBRIC

After each reading, you will participate in a group activity or discussion with your peers. You may be provided speaking frames to guide your discussions or writing frames to support your group work. To complete these activities, you should revisit the excerpt for textual evidence and support. When you finish, use the Self-Assessment Rubric to evaluate how well you participated and collaborated.

# EXTENDED WRITING PROJECT

The Extended Writing Project is your opportunity to explore the theme of each unit in a longer written work. You will draw information from your readings, research, and own life experiences to complete the assignment.

## 1 WRITING PROJECT

After you have read all of the unit text selections, you will move on to a writing project. Each project will guide you through the process of writing an argumentative, narrative, informative, or literary analysis essay. Student models and graphic organizers will provide guidance and help you organize your thoughts as you plan and write your essay. Throughout the project, you will also study and work on specific writing skills to help you develop different portions of your writing.

## 2 WRITING PROCESS STEPS

There are five steps in the writing process: **Prewrite**, **Plan**, **Draft**, **Revise**, and **Edit, Proofread, and Publish**. During each step, you will form and shape your writing project so that you can effectively express your ideas. Lessons focus on one step at a time, and you will have the chance to receive feedback from your peers and teacher.

## 3 WRITING SKILLS

Each Writing Skill lesson focuses on a specific strategy or technique that you will use during your writing project. The lessons begin by analyzing a student model or mentor text, and give you a chance to learn and practice the skill on its own. Then, you will have the opportunity to apply each new skill to improve the writing in your own project.

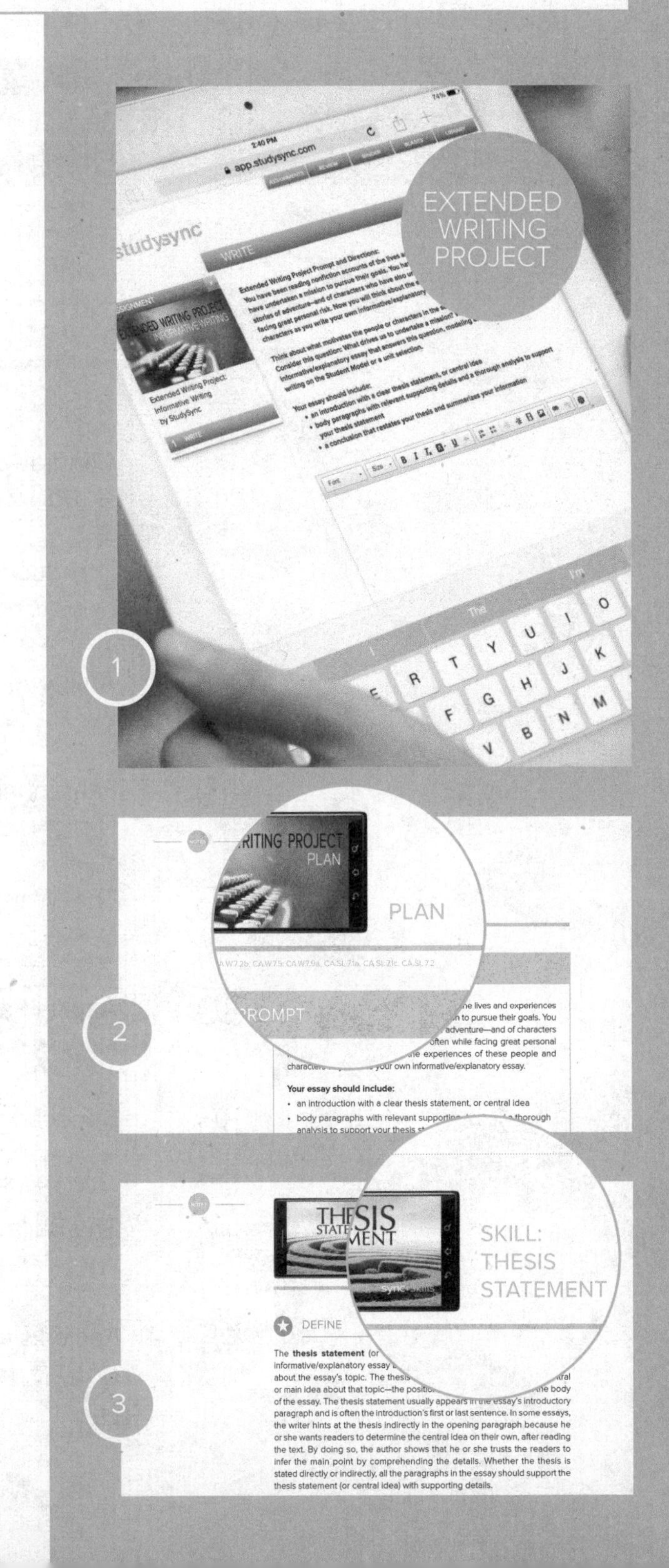

UNIT 2 When is it appropriate to challenge the rules?

# Taking a Stand

## TEXTS

## ENGLISH LANGUAGE DEVELOPMENT TEXTS

## EXTENDED WRITING PROJECT

## INTRODUCTION

studysync tv

The French philosopher Voltaire first published *Candide* in 1759 during the Age of Enlightenment. Famed for his defenses of civil liberties, Voltaire wrote this work as a satire, a commentary on Liebnizian optimism, a belief that the world is perfect—the best of all possible places. Having experienced such historical events as the Seven Years War and the 1755 Lisbon Earthquake, Voltaire was prompted to write this short novel in which he ridicules religion, theologians, governments, armies, and philosophers through the allegorical story of the naïve Candide. Published to both great success and scandal, this story of innocence and love is taught more than any other work of French literature. In this excerpt from the beginning of the book we are introduced to our good-hearted protagonist.

# "Candide listened attentively and believed innocently..."

## FIRST READ

*Excerpt from Chapter I*

HOW CANDIDE WAS BROUGHT UP IN A MAGNIFICENT CASTLE, AND HOW HE WAS EXPELLED THENCE.

1 In a castle of Westphalia, belonging to the Baron of Thunder-ten-Tronckh, lived a youth, whom nature had endowed with the most gentle manners. His countenance was a true picture of his soul. He combined a true judgment with simplicity of spirit, which was the reason, I apprehend, of his being called Candide. The old servants of the family suspected him to have been the son of the Baron's sister, by a good, honest gentleman of the neighborhood, whom that young lady would never marry because he had been able to prove only seventy-one quarterings, the rest of his genealogical tree having been lost through the injuries of time.

2 The Baron was one of the most powerful lords in Westphalia, for his castle had not only a gate, but windows. His great hall, even, was hung with tapestry. All the dogs of his farm-yards formed a pack of hounds at need; his grooms were his huntsmen; and the curate of the village was his grand almoner. They called him "My Lord," and laughed at all his stories.

3 The Baron's lady weighed about three hundred and fifty pounds, and was therefore a person of great consideration, and she did the honours of the house with a dignity that commanded still greater respect. Her daughter Cunégonde was seventeen years of age, fresh-coloured, comely, plump, and desirable. The Baron's son seemed to be in every respect worthy of his father. The Preceptor Pangloss was the oracle of the family, and little Candide heard his lessons with all the good faith of his age and character.

4 Pangloss was professor of metaphysico-theologico-cosmolo-nigology. He proved admirably that there is no effect without a cause, and that, in this best of all possible worlds, the Baron's castle was the most magnificent of castles, and his lady the best of all possible Baronesses.

5 "It is **demonstrable,**" said he, "that things cannot be otherwise than as they are; for all being created for an end, all is necessarily for the best end. Observe, that the nose has been formed to bear spectacles—thus we have spectacles. Legs are visibly designed for stockings—and we have stockings. Stones were made to be hewn, and to construct castles—therefore my lord has a magnificent castle; for the greatest baron in the province ought to be the best lodged. Pigs were made to be eaten—therefore we eat pork all the year round. Consequently they who assert that all is well have said a foolish thing, they should have said all is for the best."

6 Candide listened attentively and believed innocently; for he thought Miss Cunégonde extremely beautiful, though he never had the courage to tell her so. He concluded that after the happiness of being born of Baron of Thunder-ten-Tronckh, the second degree of happiness was to be Miss Cunégonde, the third that of seeing her every day, and the fourth that of hearing Master Pangloss, the greatest philosopher of the whole province, and **consequently** of the whole world.

7 One day Cunégonde, while walking near the castle, in a little wood which they called a park, saw between the bushes, Dr. Pangloss giving a lesson in experimental natural philosophy to her mother's chamber-maid, a little brown wench, very pretty and very **docile**. As Miss Cunégonde had a great disposition for the sciences, she breathlessly observed the repeated experiments of which she was a witness; she clearly perceived the force of the Doctor's reasons, the effects, and the causes; she turned back greatly flurried, quite pensive, and filled with the desire to be **learned;** dreaming that she might well be a sufficient reason for young Candide, and he for her.

8 She met Candide on reaching the castle and blushed; Candide blushed also; she wished him good morrow in a faltering tone, and Candide spoke to her without knowing what he said. The next day after dinner, as they went from table, Cunégonde and Candide found themselves behind a screen; Cunégonde let fall her handkerchief, Candide picked it up, she took him innocently by the hand, the youth as innocently kissed the young lady's hand with particular **vivacity** sensibility, and grace; their lips met, their eyes sparkled, their knees trembled, their hands strayed. Baron Thunder-ten-Tronckh passed near the screen and beholding this cause and effect chased Candide

from the castle with great kicks on the backside; Cunégonde fainted away; she was boxed on the ears by the Baroness, as soon as she came to herself; and all was consternation in this most magnificent and most agreeable of all possible castles.

## THINK QUESTIONS CA-CCSS: CA.RL.9-10.1, CA.L.9-10.4d

1. Candide's name comes from the Latin word *candidus,* meaning "white," to connote purity and innocence. Describe what qualities the main character has that make his name, "Candide," appropriate. What textual evidence supports your answers?

2. What does Candide admire about the Baron's castle? Why is Candide envious as a result? Cite evidence from the text to support your answer.

3. Why does the Baron throw Candide out of his home? How does this plot event relate to the statement that this is "the best of all possible worlds"?

4. Based on your knowledge of Greek and Latin roots, what do you think someone who studies *metaphisico-theologico-cosmolo-nigology* knows a lot about? Explain how you determined your answer. Why do you think Voltaire created such a subject in this novel?

5. We usually see the word **learned** as a verb, as in "I learned my lesson that day." How can you tell that it is an adjective in this passage?

# CLOSE READ

CA-CCSS: CA.RL.9-10.1, CA.RL.9-10.2, CA.RL.9-10.3, CA.RL.9-10.6, CA.L.9-10.5a, CA.W.9-10.1a, CA.W.9-10.1b, CA.W.9-10.4, CA.W.9-10.5, CA.W.9-10.6, CA.W.9-10.9a, CA.W.9-10.10

Reread the excerpt from *Candide*. As you reread, complete the Focus Questions below. Then use your answers and annotations from the questions to help you complete the Writing Prompt.

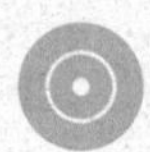

## FOCUS QUESTIONS

1. Highlight text in the first paragraph where the narrator reveals the thoughts of the old servants about the Baron's sister and Candide. Why does the narrator include these details? Make annotations to explain what these details suggest about the narrator's point of view.

2. Use the annotation tool to discuss what Candide thinks will make him happiest in the world. What does this show about Candide's character? Highlight text evidence that supports your answer.

3. Highlight the phrase "experimental natural philosophy" in Paragraph 7. Make an annotation to explain this figure of speech and why you think Voltaire used figurative language to describe the situation. Highlight one or two other examples of figurative language and annotate to explain the effect of these on the storytelling.

4. Reread Paragraph 5. Then highlight textual evidence and make annotations to indicate how Pangloss's phrase in Paragraph 4, "the best of all possible worlds," applies to the Baron and his castle. What does the passage reveal about Pangloss's philosophy and his notions of cause and effect? Annotate to explain your answer.

5. Identify the "cause and effect" mentioned in the last paragraph. What rule has Candide challenged? Does he understand what he has done? Finally, is Candide living in the "best of all possible worlds"? Annotate to explain your answer. Highlight evidence from the last paragraphs of the excerpt to support your explanation.

6. Look at the word **faltering** in the last paragraph. Identify its part of speech. Based on the part of speech and context clues in the sentence, what do you think "faltering" means? Highlight evidence in the sentence and make annotations to explain your answer.

## WRITING PROMPT

Dr. Pangloss tells Candide that he lives in the "best of all possible worlds," but the narrator offers details that might not support that point of view. Think about how you visualize the world. Do you agree with Pangloss's philosophy? Write a 300-word essay to argue for or against this world view, using details from the text to help you discuss your ideas

# INTRODUCTION TO ANTIGONE

**NON-FICTION**

Bernard Knox

1982

## INTRODUCTION

In *Antigone*, the Greek playwright Sophocles writes about Oedipus's daughter Antigone and her desire to bury the body of her brother Polynices, who has died fighting in a civil war. In order to fulfill her family duty, Antigone will need to defy the new ruler, Creon, who believes that Polynices was a traitor and has forbidden Antigone and her sister Ismene from honoring him with a burial. The excerpt below from Bernard Knox's introduction to the play provides background on the ancient Greek customs that underlie the conflict.

# "Denial of burial in their homeland to traitors...was not unknown in Greece."

## FIRST READ

*From: "Antigone"*

1 [Creon] represents a viewpoint few Greeks would have challenged: that in times of crisis, the supreme loyalty of the citizen is to the state and its duly **constituted** authorities.

2 It is important to remember this since the natural instinct of all modern readers and playgoers is to sympathize fully with Antigone, the rebel and martyr. This is of course a correct instinct; in the end the gods, through their spokesman, the prophet Tiresias, uphold her claim that divine law does indeed prescribe burial for all dead men. But though she appeals to this law—"the great unwritten, unshakable traditions" (505)—in her magnificent challenge to Creon, she has other motives too. She proclaims again and again, to her sister Ismene as to her opponent Creon, the duty she owes to her brother, to the family relationship. "If I had allowed / my own mother's son to rot, an unburied corpse"—she tells the king, "that would have been an agony!" (520–22). "He is my brother," she tells her sister Ismene, "and—deny it as you will— / your brother too" (55–56). Creon's denial of burial to the corpse of Polynices has assaulted this fierce devotion to blood relationship at a particularly sensitive point, for the funeral rites, especially the emotional lament over the dead, were, in an ancient Greek household, the duty and privilege of the women. (In the villages of Greece today they still are.) Antigone and Ismene are the last surviving women of the house of Oedipus; this is why it seems to Antigone that Creon's decree is aimed particularly at them—"the martial law our good Creon / lays down for you and me" (37–38)—and why she takes it for granted Ismene will help her and turns so **contemptuously** and harshly against her when she refuses.

...

NOTES

3 Antigone appeals not only to the bond of kindred blood but also to the unwritten law, **sanctioned** by the gods, that the dead must be given proper burial—a religious principle. But Creon's position is not anti-religious; in fact he believes that he has religion on his side. The gods, for him, are the gods of the city, which contains and protects their shrines, celebrates their festivals and sacrifices, and prays to them for **deliverance;** Creon finds it unthinkable that these gods should demand the burial of a traitor to the city who came with a foreign army at his back

to burn their temples ringed with pillars,
. . . scorch their hallowed earth
and fling their laws to the winds. (323–25)

4 Once again, there would have been many in the audience who felt the same way. These vivid phrases would have recalled to them the **destruction** of Athens and the desecration of its temples by the Persian invaders in 480; they would have had no second thoughts about denying burial to the corpse of any Athenian who had fought on the Persian side. Denial of burial in their homeland to traitors, real or supposed, was not unknown in Greece.

---

Excerpted from *The Three Theban Plays: Antigone; Oedipus the King; Oedipus at Colonus* by Sophocles, Robert Fagles (Translator) and Bernard Knox (Introduction), published by the Penguin Group.

## THINK QUESTIONS

CA-CCSS: CA.RI.9-10.1, CA.RI.9-10.4, CA.L.9-10.4a, CA.L.9-10.4b

1. According to Knox, what is the difference between Creon's beliefs and Antigone's beliefs regarding the burial of Polynices' corpse ? How does this difference help set up the action of the play? Explain how ancient Greeks would have regarded the conflict, as opposed to modern theatergoers. Cite evidence from the text to support your answer.

2. Briefly summarize Antigone's argument that as Polynices' sister, she has a right to demand that he be buried. Cite evidence from the text to support your answer.

3. According to Knox, why wouldn't Creon have second thoughts about denying burial rights to a traitor? Why might the Greeks of Sophocles's time agree with Creon? Provide a quotation from the text that supports your response.

4. Use context to determine the meaning of the word **contemptuously** as it is used at the end of the second paragraph in "Introduction to *Antigone.*" Write an explanation of how you used the clues, and then your definition of "contemptuously" here.

5. Recall that the word *consecrate* comes from the Latin *consecrare,* meaning "sacred," and that "consecrate" means "to honor or to make sacred." The Latin prefix *de-* means "apart, away, off, or from." Use your understanding of Latin roots and affixes as well as context clues in the passage to determine the meaning of **desecration** in the last paragraph. Write your explanation and your definition of "desecration" here.

## CLOSE READ

CA-CCSS: CA.RI.9-10.1, CA.RI.9-10.3, CA.RI.9-10.5, CA.W.9-10.4, CA.W.9-10.5, CA.W.9-10.6, CA.W.9-10.9b, CA.W.9-10.10

Reread the excerpt from *Introduction to Antigone*. As you reread, complete the Focus Questions below. Then use your answers and annotations from the questions to help you complete the Writing Prompt.

### FOCUS QUESTIONS

1. According to Knox, what is the cause of Antigone's anger toward Creon? What are the possible effects of this on herself and those around her? Highlight textual evidence in the excerpt to support your ideas. Write annotations to explain your choices.
2. How does compare-and-contrast text structure of the essay help readers understand the different points of view in the play *Antigone*? Highlight evidence in the text and write annotations to explain your choices.
3. What connections does Knox draw between Antigone's personality, her beliefs, and her actions? How does he develop his claims? Highlight textual evidence and write annotations to explain your idea.
4. Knox states that Antigone believes that Creon's decision not to let Polynices be buried is aimed at her and her sister personally. How does his analysis support his ideas? Highlight your evidence and make annotations that support your understanding.
5. Based on the ways Knox compares and contrasts the points of view in the play *Antigone* in this excerpt, does he think that Antigone has the right to challenge the rule of law set down by Creon? Highlight textual evidence in the paragraph and use the annotation tool to support your answer.

### WRITING PROMPT

Use your understanding of key ideas, organizational structure, and point of view to explain how Knox's "Introduction to *Antigone*" might enhance your reading of the library excerpt from the play, *Antigone*. How does Bernard Knox's analysis of the play and explanation of cultural history help you understand the central conflict of *Antigone*, as well as the characters? Cite textual evidence to support your response.

# ANTIGONE

**DRAMA**

Sophocles
circa 441 BCE

## INTRODUCTION

Born around 497 BCE, Sophocles was one of the three great dramatists from Ancient Greece whose plays survived to modern times. *Antigone* is one of his "Theban" plays, three tragedies that focus on the fate of the city-state Thebes during and after the reign of the mythical King Oedipus. In the play, Antigone's two brothers have killed each other in battle. Antigone wants to honor each of them, but her uncle, Creon, the new king, has forbidden it. In this passage, she asks her sister, Ismene, for help.

# "Go thine own way; myself will bury him."

## FIRST READ

1 [ANTIGONE *and* ISMENE *before the Palace gates.*]

2 ANTIGONE: Ismene, sister of my blood and heart,
3 See'st thou how Zeus would in our lives fulfill
4 The weird of Oedipus, a world of woes!
5 For what of pain, affliction, outrage, shame,
6 Is lacking in our fortunes, thine and mine?
7 What can its purport be? Didst hear and heed,
8 Or art thou deaf when friends are banned as foes?

9 ISMENE: To me, Antigone, no word of friends
10 Has come, or glad or **grievous,** since we twain
11 Were reft of our two brethren in one day
12 By double fratricide; and since i' the night
13 Our Argive leaguers fled, no later news
14 Has reached me, to inspirit or deject.

15 ANTIGONE: I know 'twas so, and therefore summoned thee
16 Beyond the gates to breathe it in thine ear.

17 ISMENE: What is it? Some dark secret stirs thy breast.

18 ANTIGONE: What but the thought of our two brothers dead,
19 The one by Creon graced with funeral rites,
20 The other disappointed? Eteocles
21 He hath consigned to earth (as fame reports)
22 With obsequies that use and wont ordain,
23 So gracing him among the dead below.
24 But Polyneices, a dishonored corse,
25 (So by report the royal **edict** runs)
26 No man may bury him or make lament—

NOTES

27 Must leave him tombless and unwept, a feast
28 For kites to scent afar and swoop upon.
29 Such is the edict (if report speak true)
30 Of Creon, our most noble Creon, aimed
31 At thee and me, aye me too; and anon
32 He will be here to **promulgate,** for such
33 As have not heard, his mandate; 'tis in sooth
34 No passing humor, for the edict says
35 Whoe'er transgresses shall be stoned to death.
36 So stands it with us; now 'tis thine to show
37 If thou art worthy of thy blood or **base**.

38 ISMENE: But how, my rash, fond sister, in such case
39 Can I do anything to make or mar?

40 ANTIGONE: Say, wilt thou aid me and abet? Decide.

41 ISMENE: In what bold venture? What is in thy thought?

42 ANTIGONE: Lend me a hand to bear the corpse away.

43 ISMENE: What, bury him despite the interdict?

44 ANTIGONE: My brother, and, though thou deny him, thine.
45 No man shall say that *I* betrayed a brother.

46 ISMENE: Wilt thou persist, though Creon has forbid?

47 ANTIGONE: What right has he to keep me from my own?

48 ISMENE: Bethink thee, sister, of our father's fate,
49 Abhorred, dishonored, self-convinced of sin,
50 Blinded, himself his executioner.
51 Think of his mother-wife (ill sorted names)
52 Done by a noose herself had twined to death;
53 And last, our hapless brethren in one day,
54 Both in a mutual destiny involved,
55 Self-slaughtered, both the slayer and the slain.
56 Bethink thee, sister, we are left alone;
57 Shall we not perish wretchedest of all,
58 If in defiance of the law we cross
59 A monarch's will? —Weak women, think of that,
60 Not framed by nature to contend with men.
61 Remember this too that the stronger rules;
62 We must obey his orders, these or worse.

63 Therefore I plead compulsion and entreat
64 The dead to pardon. I perforce obey
65 The powers that be. 'Tis foolishness, I ween,
66 To overstep in aught the golden mean.

67 ANTIGONE: I urge no more; nay, wert thou willing still,
68 I would not welcome such a fellowship.
69 Go thine own way; myself will bury him.
70 How sweet to die in such employ, to rest—
71 Sister and brother linked in love's embrace—
72 A sinless sinner, banned awhile on earth,
73 But by the dead commended; and with them
74 I shall abide for ever. As for thee,
75 Scorn, if thou wilt, the eternal laws of Heaven.

76 ISMENE: I scorn them not, but to defy the State
77 Or break her ordinance I have no skill.

78 ANTIGONE: A **specious** pretext. I will go alone
79 To lap my dearest brother in the grave.

80 ISMENE: My poor, fond sister, how I fear for thee!

81 ANTIGONE: O waste no fears on me; look to thyself.

82 ISMENE: At least let no man know of thine intent,
83 But keep it close and secret, as will I.

84 ANTIGONE: O tell it, sister; I shall hate thee more
85 If thou proclaim it not to all the town.

86 ISMENE: Thou hast a fiery soul for numbing work.

87 ANTIGONE: I pleasure those whom I would liefest please.

88 ISMENE: If thou succeed; but thou art doomed to fail.

89 ANTIGONE: When strength shall fail me, yes, but not before.

90 ISMENE: But, if the venture's hopeless, why essay?

91 ANTIGONE: Sister, forbear, or I shall hate thee soon,
92 And the dead man will hate thee too, with cause.
93 Say I am mad and give my madness rein
94 To wreck itself; the worst that can befall
95 Is but to die an honorable death.

96 ISMENE: Have thine own way then; 'tis a mad endeavor,
97 Yet to thy lovers thou art dear as ever. [*Exeunt*]

## THINK QUESTIONS CA-CCSS: CA.RL.9-10.1, CA.L.9-10.4a

1. What is the relationship between Antigone and Ismene? What are they discussing as this excerpt from the play opens? Cite textual evidence to demonstrate your understanding.
2. Who is Creon? How does Antigone feel about him? Cite textual evidence to demonstrate your understanding.
3. What is Antigone's plan, and what is Ismene's response? Cite textual evidence and explain your understanding.
4. Use context to determine the meaning of the word **edict** as it is used in Antigone's first long speech. Write your explanation of the context clues and then write your definition here.
5. Antigone tells her sister, "'Tis thine to show/If thou art worthy of thy blood or base." The word *or* tells you that *base* is being contrasted with *worthy of thy blood.* Given that, what do you suppose **base** means? Write your ideas here.

# CLOSE READ

CA-CCSS: CA.RL.9-10.1, CA.RL.9-10.3, CA.RL.9-10.4, CA.RL.9-10.6, CA.W.9-10.4, CA.W.9-10.5, CA.W.9-10.6, CA.W.9-10.9a, CA.W.9-10.10

Reread *Antigone*. As you reread, complete the Focus Questions below. Then use your answers and annotations from the questions to help you complete the Writing Prompt.

## FOCUS QUESTIONS

1. What does Creon's treatment of Polyneices tell you about the culture in which Antigone lives? Highlight textual evidence that supports your understanding. Write annotations to explain your ideas.

2. Think about the language Ismene uses to describe Antigone's plans. What does this use of language say about Ismene and her view of the society she lives in? Highlight textual evidence to demonstrate the way Ismene uses language. Write annotations to explain your ideas.

3. Based on this scene from the play, what do you know about Antigone's character? Highlight lines from the text, including what she says herself and what is said about her, to demonstrate your understanding. Write annotations to explain your ideas.

4. How does Antigone's attitude toward her sister change over the course of the scene? What does this shift reveal about both of their characters? Highlight lines or phrases that indicate the changes in attitude. Write annotations to explain your ideas.

5. Why does Antigone believe she is right to challenge Creon's rule? Highlight textual evidence that points out the causes of their cultural clash, and then write annotations to explain your ideas.

## WRITING PROMPT

Imagine you are Antigone. What do you want for your brother, what do you want for yourself, and why are you so determined to defy Creon? Examine your motives in a private journal entry of at least 300 words. Make sure your writing reflects the character of Antigone as depicted in Sophocles's play. Refer to the play to collect ideas and to develop an appropriate tone for your journal entry.

# FAHRENHEIT 451

**FICTION**

Ray Bradbury

1953

## INTRODUCTION

studysync tv

Guy Montag is a fireman. However, in the world of Ray Bradbury's futuristic novel, *Fahrenheit 451*, firemen do not put out fires; they set them. And what they burn, in this anti-intellectual society, are books—a tradition Montag seems more than willing to uphold. In this excerpt from the beginning of the novel, the fireman is walking home from a day of burning, his senses alert to the sounds and smells of the night. Then he encounters Clarisse, an unusual young woman whose naïve questions unsettle his status quo and challenge the values

# "It was a pleasure to burn."

## FIRST READ

*Excerpt from Part 1: "The Hearth and the Salamander"*

1 It was a pleasure to burn.

2 It was a special pleasure to see things eaten, to see things blackened and changed. With the brass nozzle in his fists, with this great python spitting its venomous kerosene upon the world, the blood pounded in his head, and his hands were the hands of some amazing conductor playing all the symphonies of blazing and burning to bring down the tatters and charcoal ruins of history. With his symbolic helmet numbered 451 on his **stolid** head, and his eyes all orange flame with the thought of what came next, he flicked the igniter and the house jumped up in a gorging fire that burned the evening sky red and yellow and black. He strode in a swarm of fireflies. He wanted above all, like the old joke, to shove a marshmallow on a stick in the furnace, while the flapping pigeon-winged books died on the porch and lawn of the house. While the books went up in sparkling whirls and blew away on a wind turned dark with burning.

3 Montag grinned the fierce grin of all men singed and driven back by flame.

4 He knew that when he returned to the firehouse, he might wink at himself, a minstrel man, burnt-corked, in the mirror. Later, going to sleep, he would feel the fiery smile still gripped by his face muscles, in the dark. It never went away, that smile, it never ever went away, as long as he remembered.

5 He hung up his black beetle-colored helmet and shined it; he hung his flameproof jacket neatly; he showered **luxuriously,** and then, whistling, hands in pockets, walked across the upper floor of the fire station and fell down the hole. At the last moment, when disaster seemed positive, he pulled his hands from his pockets and broke his fall by grasping the golden pole. He slid to a squeaking halt, the heels one inch from the concrete floor downstairs.

6 He walked out of the fire station and along the midnight street toward the subway where the silent air-propelled train slid soundlessly down its lubricated flue in the earth and let him out with a great puff of warm air onto the cream-tiled escalator rising to the suburb.

7 Whistling, he let the escalator waft him into the still night air. He walked toward the corner, thinking little at all about nothing in particular. Before he reached the corner, however, he slowed as if a wind had sprung up from nowhere, as if someone had called his name.

8 The last few nights he had had the most uncertain feelings about the sidewalk just around the corner here, moving in the starlight toward his house. He had felt that a moment prior to his making the turn, someone had been there.

• • •

9 "Do you mind if I walk back with you? I'm Clarisse McClellan."

10 "Clarisse. Guy Montag. Come along. What are you doing out so late wandering around? How old are you?"

11 They walked in the warm-cool blowing night on the silvered pavement and there was the faintest breath of fresh apricots and strawberries in the air, and he looked around and realized this was quite impossible, so late in the year.

12 There was only the girl walking with him now, her face bright as snow in the moonlight, and he knew she was working his questions around, seeking the best answers she could possibly give.

13 "Well," she said, "I'm seventeen and I'm crazy. My uncle says the two always go together. When people ask your age, he said, always say seventeen and insane. Isn't this a nice time of night to walk? I like to smell things and look at things, and sometimes stay up all night, walking, and watch the sun rise."

14 They walked on again in silence and finally she said, thoughtfully, "You know, I'm not afraid of you at all."

15 He was surprised. "Why should you be?"

16 "So many people are. Afraid of firemen, I mean. But you're just a man, after all . . ."

17 He saw himself in her eyes, suspended in two shining drops of bright water, himself dark and tiny, in fine detail, the lines about his mouth, everything there, as if her eyes were two miraculous bits of violet amber that might capture and hold him intact. Her face, turned to him now, was fragile milk

crystal with a soft and constant light in it. It was not the **hysterical** light of electricity but—what? But the strangely comfortable and rare and gently flattering light of the candle. One time, as a child, in a power failure, his mother had found and lit a last candle and there had been a brief hour of **rediscovery,** of such illumination that space lost its vast dimensions and grew comfortably around them, and they, mother and son, alone, transformed, hoping that the power might not come on again too soon . . .

18 And then Clarisse McClellan said:

19 "Do you mind if I ask? How long've you worked at being a fireman?"

20 "Since I was twenty, ten years ago."

21 "Do you ever read any of the books you burn?"

22 He laughed. "That's against the law!"

23 "Oh. Of course."

24 "It's fine work. Monday burn Millay, Wednesday Whitman, Friday Faulkner, burn 'em to ashes, then burn the ashes. That's our official slogan."

25 They walked still farther and the girl said, "Is it true that long ago firemen put fires out instead of going to start them?"

26 "No. Houses have always been fireproof, take my word for it."

27 "Strange. I heard once that a long time ago houses used to burn by accident and they needed firemen to stop the flames."

28 He laughed.

29 She glanced quickly over. "Why are you laughing?"

30 "I don't know." He started to laugh again and stopped. "Why?"

31 "You laugh when I haven't been funny and you answer right off. You never stop to think what I've asked you."

---

Excerpted from *Fahrenheit 451* by Ray Bradbury, published by Simon & Schuster.

## THINK QUESTIONS CA-CCSS: CA.RL.9-10.1, CA.L.9-10.4a

1. At what point in time is this novel set, and how can you tell? Cite textual evidence to explain your answer.

2. Who is Guy Montag and what do you know about him? Cite textual evidence to explain your response as well as details that help you visualize his job.

3. Write two or three sentences explaining why you think Clarisse is talking to Montag. What do you think is her motivation for asking these particular questions? Cite textual evidence to explain your inferences or predictions.

4. Use context, including antonyms, to determine the meaning of the word **hysterical** as it is used in *Fahrenheit 451*. Write your definition of hysterical here.

5. The word **stolid** comes from the Latin root stolidus, meaning "dull or stupid." Read the word as it is used in the excerpt:

   "With his symbolic helmet numbered 451 on his **stolid** head, and his eyes all orange flame with the thought of what came next, he flicked the igniter and the house jumped up in a gorging fire that burned the evening sky red and yellow and black."

   Using the Latin root to determine the meaning, what does the word **stolid** tell readers about Montag?

# CLOSE READ

CA-CCSS: CA.RL.9-10.1, CA.RL.9-10.3, CA.RL.9-10.4, CA.L.9-10.5a, CA.RI.9-10.1, CA.W.9-10.4, CA.W.9-10.5, CA.W.9-10.6, CA.W.9-10.9b, CA.W.9-10.10

Reread the excerpt from *Fahrenheit 451*. As you reread, complete the Focus Questions below. Then use your answers and annotations from the questions to help you complete the Writing Prompt.

## FOCUS QUESTIONS

1. As you reread the excerpt from *Fahrenheit 451*, highlight several words and phrases that have negative or positive connotations. What inferences can you draw about Montag and the world he lives in based on these connotations? Use the annotation tool to explain both the connotations and the inferences you made.

2. In paragraphs 6 and 7, the author describes Montag's walk home from work. Highlight places where the structure of the sentences and the use of figurative language help to show Montag's reliance on technology and other people to direct him. What does this reveal about the world of the novel? Write annotations to explain your choices.

3. Reread the dialogue between Montag and Clarisse in paragraphs 21-31. How does this exchange between the two characters connect with Bradbury's description of Montag in the seventh paragraph? Write annotations to explain what the dialogue and description reveal about Montag's character, and how it reflects on the fact that books have been banned in this future society.

4. Think about the narrator of *Fahrenheit 451* and his or her relationship to the characters and events. What is his or her point of view, and how does it reveal the main character? Highlight textual evidence over the course of the narrative to support your ideas and write annotations to explain your choices.

5. Think about the last section of the excerpt. What sort of challenge to the rules of this future society do Clarisse's questions introduce into the story? How does Montag feel about the appropriateness of this challenge? Cite evidence from the text to support your answer.

## WRITING PROMPT

Based on your understanding of figurative language, tone, and the characters in the excerpt, what can you infer about the society in which Montag and Clarisse live? What can you infer about the two characters and what makes them interested in each other? Finally, what predictions might you make about what might take place in the rest of the novel? Cite textual evidence to support your ideas.

# THE WHISPERERS:

## PRIVATE LIFE IN STALIN'S RUSSIA

**NON-FICTION**

Orlando Figes
2007

## INTRODUCTION

From the 1920s to the 1950s, a reign of terror gripped the Soviet Union under Josef Stalin. This book by British historian Orlando Figes goes beyond the show trials, executions, and gulag imprisonments to tell the stories of ordinary citizens in Stalinist Russia, who dared not speak above a whisper for fear of reprisals. The excerpt here concerns the persecution of "kulaks"—peasants who prospered by working outside the confines of the *kolkhoz* (collective farm).

# "What were the motives of the men and women who carried out this brutal war against the peasantry?"

## FIRST READ

1 One Klavdiia Rublyova was born in 1913, the third of eleven children in a peasant family in the Irbei region of Krasnoiarsk in Siberia. Her mother died in 1924, while giving birth, leaving her father, Ilia, to bring up all the children on his own. An **enterprising** man, Ilia took advantage of the NEP [New Economic Policy] to branch out from farming to market gardening. He grew poppy seeds and cucumbers, which could easily be tended by his young children. For this he was branded a 'kulak', arrested and imprisoned, and later sent to a labour camp, leaving his children in the care of Klavdiia, who was then aged just seventeen. The children were deprived of all their father's property: the house, which he had built, was taken over by the village Soviet, while the horses, cows and sheep and the farm tools were transferred to the kolkhoz. For several weeks, the children lived in the bath-house, until officials came to take them all away to an orphanage. Klavdiia ran off with the youngest child to Kansk, near Krasnoiarsk, where her grown-up sister Raisa lived. Before they went they sold their last possessions to the other villagers. "We had nothing much to sell, we were just children," Klavdiia recalls. There was a fur-lined blanket and an old sheepskin, a feather mattress, and a mirror, which somehow we had rescued from our house. That was all we had to sell.

2 What were the motives of the men and women who carried out this brutal war against the peasantry? Most of the collectivizers were conscripted soldiers and workers — people anxious to carry out orders from above (and in some cases, to line their pockets). Hatred of the 'kulaks' had been drummed into them by their commanders and by propaganda which portrayed the 'kulak parasites' and 'bloodsuckers' as dangerous 'enemies of the people'. We were trained to see the kulaks, not as human beings, but as vermin, lice, which had to be destroyed,' recalls one young activist, the leader of a Komsomol brigade in the Kuban. 'Without the kolkhoz,' wrote another collectivizer in the 1980s, 'the kulaks would have grabbed us by the throat and skinned us all alive!'

NOTES

3 Others were carried away by their Communist enthusiasm. Inspired by the romantic revolutionary passions stirred up by the propaganda of the Five Year Plan, they believed with the Bolsheviks that any miracle could be achieved by sheer human will. As one student in those years recalls: 'We were convinced that we were creating a Communist society, that it would be achieved by the Five Year Plans, and we were ready for any sacrifice.' Today, it is easy to underestimate the emotional force of those messianic hopes and the **fanaticism** that it **engendered,** particularly in the younger generation, which had been brought up on the 'cult of struggle' and the romance of the Civil War. These young people wanted to believe that it was their calling to carry on the fight, in the words of the 'Internationale', for a 'new and better life'. In the words of one of the '25,000ers' — the urban army of enthusiasts sent into the countryside to help carry out the collectivization campaign: 'Constant struggle, struggle, and more struggle! This was how we had been taught to think — that nothing was achieved without struggle, which was a norm of social life.

4 According to this militant world-view, the creation of a new society would involve and indeed **necessitate** a bitter struggle with the forces of the old society (a logic reinforced by the propaganda of the Five Year Plan, with its constant talk of 'campaigns,' 'battles' and 'offensives' on the social, economic, international and internal 'fronts'). In this way the Communist idealists reconciled the 'anti-kulak' terror with their own utopian beliefs. Some were appalled by the brutal violence. Some were even sickened by their own role in it. But they all knew what they were doing (they could not plead that they were ignorant or that they were simply 'following orders'). And they all believed that the end justified the means.

5 Lev Kopelev, a young Communist who took part in some of the worst atrocities against the Ukrainian peasants, explained how he rationalized his actions. Kopelev had volunteered for a Komsomol brigade which requisitioned grain from the 'kulaks' in 1932. They took everything down to the last loaf of bread. Looking back on the experience in the 1970s, Kopelev recalled the children's screams and the appearance of the peasant men –'frightened, pleading, hateful, dully impassive, extinguished with despair or flaring up with half-mad daring ferocity':

6 It was excruciating to see and hear all this. And even worse to take part in it . . . And I persuaded myself, explained to myself. I mustn't give in to **debilitating** pity. We were realizing historical necessity. We were performing our revolutionary duty. We were obtaining grain for the socialist fatherland. For the Five Year Plan.

Excerpted from *The Whisperers: Private Life in Stalin's Russia* by Orlando Figes, published by Henry Holt and Company.

## THINK QUESTIONS CA-CCSS: CA.RI.9-10.1, CA.L.9-10.4a, CA.L.9-10.4b, CA.L.9-10.4d

1. Use details in the title and text to determine in what time and place the events described in this passage took place. Summarize who was affected by these events and why.

2. Use details from the text to explain how propaganda shaped the collectivizers' perceptions of the peasants and motivated their aggressive actions against these people.

3. The author indicates that the collectivizers believed that "the end justified the means." Explain the meaning of this expression as it applies to the collectivizers and use details from the text to explain why they believed in it.

4. Determine the meaning of the word **enterprising** as it is used in the first paragraph of the text and explain how context clues helped you arrive at this definition.

5. Use your understanding of the word **necessary** and your knowledge of the verb suffix *-ate,* which means "to cause to be affected by," to determine the meaning and part of speech of the word **necessitate.** Check the meaning you arrive at in context and then in a print or digital dictionary.

# CLOSE READ

CA-CCSS: CA.RI.9-10.1, CA.RI.9-10.2, CA.RI.9-10.6, CA.W.9-10.1a, CA.W.9-10.1b, CA.W.9-10.2a, CA.W.9-10.2b, CA.W.9-10.4, CA.W.9-10.5, CA.W.9-10.6, CA.W.9-10.9b, CA.W.9-10.10

Reread the text excerpt from *The Whisperers: Private Life in Stalin's Russia*. As you reread, complete the Focus Questions below. Then use your answers and annotations from the questions to help you complete the Writing Prompt.

## FOCUS QUESTIONS

1. Describe the author's main point about the "kulaks" and their treatment in Stalinist Russia, as evidenced by the story of Klavdiia and her family. Highlight evidence in the first paragraph, including specific word choices, that reinforces this point and make annotations to support the details you select. Why do you think the author includes this paragraph at the beginning of the text?
2. Much of the second paragraph describes the propaganda that led the collectivizers to fear the "kulaks" and motivated their attacks upon them. However, the paragraph also suggests that there were other motivations for the collectivizers' brutal actions. Highlight and annotate the textual evidence that identifies other potential reasons for the collectivizers' treatment of the "kulaks." In what way do these motivations paint the collectivizers in a more negative light?
3. Reread the third paragraph. Do you think that the first sentence is an effective statement of the paragraph's central or main idea? Write an annotation to explain your answer and highlight details that reinforce it.
4. Note this sentence in the fourth paragraph: "In this way the Communist idealists reconciled the 'anti-kulak' terror with their own utopian beliefs." Highlight and annotate a sentence in the sixth paragraph that reinforces this central idea through a first-person quotation.
5. What attitude does the author have toward the collectivizers? To what extent does he sympathize with the position in which they found themselves in that place and time, and to what extent does he think they should have challenged the rules? Highlight and annotate details in the fourth paragraph that help convey the author's attitude.

## WRITING PROMPT

Compare the excerpts from *Fahrenheit 451* and *The Whisperers: Private Life in Stalin's Russia*. Using textual evidence from both selections, explore how both authors illustrate that the utopian visions of totalitarian states can, in practice, lead to an experience of dystopia for the people. Be sure to identify the central or main idea of each selection as it relates to this prompt.

# ANIMAL FARM

**FICTION**

George Orwell

1945

## INTRODUCTION

studysync tv

"Every line of serious work that I have written since 1936 has been written, directly or indirectly, against totalitarianism and for democratic socialism as I understand it," George Orwell said, in "Why I Write." Nowhere is this more evident than *Animal Farm*, Orwell's allegorical novella that employs the uprising led by Napoleon, a pig, to satirize the corruption and dictatorship of 1917-1944 Russia. This excerpt begins just after Napoleon has lifted his leg to urinate on Snowball's plan for a technological innovation that would modernize the farm.

# "By the time he had finished speaking, there was no doubt as to which way the vote would go."

## FIRST READ

*Excerpt from Chapter 5*

1 The whole farm was deeply divided on the subject of the windmill. Snowball did not deny that to build it would be a difficult business. Stone would have to be carried and built up into walls, then the sails would have to be made and after that there would be need for dynamos and cables. (How these were to be **procured,** Snowball did not say.) But he maintained that it could all be done in a year. And thereafter, he declared, so much labour would be saved that the animals would only need to work three days a week. Napoleon, on the other hand, argued that the great need of the moment was to increase food production, and that if they wasted time on the windmill they would all starve to death. The animals formed themselves into two **factions** under the slogan, "Vote for Snowball and the three-day week" and "Vote for Napoleon and the full manger." Benjamin was the only animal who did not side with either faction. He refused to believe either that food would become more plentiful or that the windmill would save work. Windmill or no windmill, he said, life would go on as it had always gone on--that is, badly.

2 Apart from the disputes over the windmill, there was the question of the defence of the farm. It was fully realised that though the human beings had been defeated in the Battle of the Cowshed they might make another and more determined attempt to recapture the farm and reinstate Mr. Jones. They had all the more reason for doing so because the news of their defeat had spread across the countryside and made the animals on the neighbouring farms more **restive** than ever. As usual, Snowball and Napoleon were in disagreement. According to Napoleon, what the animals must do was to procure firearms and train themselves in the use of them. According to Snowball, they must send out more and more pigeons and stir up rebellion among the animals on the other farms. The one argued that if they could not defend themselves they were bound to be conquered, the other argued that

if rebellions happened everywhere they would have no need to defend themselves. The animals listened first to Napoleon, then to Snowball, and could not make up their minds which was right; indeed, they always found themselves in agreement with the one who was speaking at the moment.

3 At last the day came when Snowball's plans were completed. At the Meeting on the following Sunday the question of whether or not to begin work on the windmill was to be put to the vote. When the animals had assembled in the big barn, Snowball stood up and, though occasionally interrupted by bleating from the sheep, set forth his reasons for advocating the building of the windmill. Then Napoleon stood up to reply. He said very quietly that the windmill was nonsense and that he advised nobody to vote for it, and promptly sat down again; he had spoken for barely thirty seconds, and seemed almost indifferent as to the effect he produced. At this Snowball sprang to his feet, and shouting down the sheep, who had begun bleating again, broke into a passionate appeal in favour of the windmill. Until now the animals had been about equally divided in their sympathies, but in a moment Snowball's eloquence had carried them away. In glowing sentences he painted a picture of Animal Farm as it might be when **sordid** labour was lifted from the animals' backs. His imagination had now run far beyond chaff-cutters and turnip-slicers. Electricity, he said, could operate threshing machines, ploughs, harrows, rollers, and reapers and binders, besides supplying every stall with its own electric light, hot and cold water, and an electric heater. By the time he had finished speaking, there was no doubt as to which way the vote would go. But just at this moment Napoleon stood up and, casting a peculiar sidelong look at Snowball, uttered a high-pitched whimper of a kind no one had ever heard him utter before.

4 At this there was a terrible baying sound outside, and nine enormous dogs wearing brass-studded collars came bounding into the barn. They dashed straight for Snowball, who only sprang from his place just in time to escape their snapping jaws. In a moment he was out of the door and they were after him. Too amazed and frightened to speak, all the animals crowded through the door to watch the chase. Snowball was racing across the long pasture that led to the road. He was running as only a pig can run, but the dogs were close on his heels. Suddenly he slipped and it seemed certain that they had him. Then he was up again, running faster than ever, then the dogs were gaining on him again. One of them all but closed his jaws on Snowball's tail, but Snowball whisked it free just in time. Then he put on an extra spurt and, with a few inches to spare, slipped through a hole in the hedge and was seen no more.

5 Silent and terrified, the animals crept back into the barn. In a moment the dogs came bounding back. At first no one had been able to imagine where these creatures came from, but the problem was soon solved: they were the

puppies whom Napoleon had taken away from their mothers and reared privately. Though not yet full-grown, they were huge dogs, and as fierce-looking as wolves. They kept close to Napoleon. It was noticed that they wagged their tails to him in the same way as the other dogs had been used to do to Mr. Jones.

6 Napoleon, with the dogs following him, now mounted on to the raised portion of the floor where Major had previously stood to deliver his speech. He announced that from now on the Sunday-morning Meetings would come to an end. They were unnecessary, he said, and wasted time. In future all questions relating to the working of the farm would be settled by a special committee of pigs, presided over by himself. These would meet in private and afterwards communicate their decisions to the others. The animals would still assemble on Sunday mornings to salute the flag, sing 'Beasts of England', and receive their orders for the week; but there would be no more debates.

7 In spite of the shock that Snowball's expulsion had given them, the animals were dismayed by this announcement. Several of them would have protested if they could have found the right arguments. Even Boxer was vaguely troubled. He set his ears back, shook his forelock several times, and tried hard to **marshal** his thoughts; but in the end he could not think of anything to say. Some of the pigs themselves, however, were more articulate. Four young porkers in the front row uttered shrill squeals of disapproval, and all four of them sprang to their feet and began speaking at once. But suddenly the dogs sitting round Napoleon let out deep, menacing growls, and the pigs fell silent and sat down again. Then the sheep broke out into a tremendous bleating of "Four legs good, two legs bad!" which went on for nearly a quarter of an hour and put an end to any chance of discussion.

8 Afterwards Squealer was sent round the farm to explain the new arrangement to the others.

9 "Comrades," he said, "I trust that every animal here appreciates the sacrifice that Comrade Napoleon has made in taking this extra labour upon himself. Do not imagine, comrades, that leadership is a pleasure! On the contrary, it is a deep and heavy responsibility. No one believes more firmly than Comrade Napoleon that all animals are equal. He would be only too happy to let you make your decisions for yourselves. But sometimes you might make the wrong decisions, comrades, and then where should we be? Suppose you had decided to follow Snowball, with his moonshine of windmills—Snowball, who, as we now know, was no better than a criminal?"

10 "He fought bravely at the Battle of the Cowshed," said somebody.

11 "Bravery is not enough," said Squealer. "Loyalty and obedience are more important. And as to the Battle of the Cowshed, I believe the time will come when we shall find that Snowball's part in it was much exaggerated."

Excerpted from *Animal Farm* by George Orwell, published by Harcourt Brace & Company.

## THINK QUESTIONS CA-CCSS: CA.RL.9-10.1, CA.L.9-10.4a

1. As the excerpt opens, who are Snowball and Napoleon, and what has led them to this point? How do you know? What is Snowball arguing for, and why? Cite textual details that support your explanation.
2. Was the attack of the dogs planned? Cite textual evidence to support your response.
3. What reason does Napoleon give for ending the Sunday meetings? Why does he really end them? Cite evidence to support your response.
4. Use context clues to determine the meaning of the word **procured** as it is used in *Animal Farm*. Write your definition of "procured" here.
5. Use context to determine the meaning of the word **factions** as it is used in *Animal Farm*. Write your definition of **factions** here.

# CLOSE READ

CA-CCSS: CA.RL.9-10.1, CA.RL.9-10.2, CA.RL.9-10.3, CA.RL.9-10.5, CA.W.9-10.4, CA.W.9-10.5, CA.W.9-10.6, CA.W.9-10.9a, CA.W.9-10.10

Reread the excerpt from *Animal Farm*, Chapter 5. As you reread, complete the Focus Questions below. Then use your answers and annotations from the questions to help you complete the Writing Prompt.

## FOCUS QUESTIONS

1. As you reread the excerpt from *Animal Farm*, think about how the author reveals the characters of Napoleon and Snowball. What do their names, as well as their actions, reveal about their characters? Highlight textual evidence, beginning in the first paragraph to support your ideas and inferences and write annotations to explain your choices.
2. How do the other animals react to Napoleon's and Snowball's differing ideas in paragraph 2 of the selection? How do the animals' reactions connect to the text's themes? Highlight evidence to support your ideas and write annotations to explain your choices.
3. In the fifth paragraph, the narrator explains the origin of Napoleon's dogs. What does this information reveal about Napoleon? Why does the author include this information at this moment? Highlight evidence to support your ideas and write annotations to explain your choices.
4. In this excerpt, only one character, Squealer, is shown to be speaking for himself through dialogue. Why do you think Orwell chose to include that character's speech while only summarizing the main points of Napoleon's and Snowball's speeches? Highlight textual evidence and write annotations to explain your ideas.
5. How did both Snowball and Napoleon challenge the existing order? What makes Snowball and Napoleon different? Use your understanding of narrative point of view and character in this selection to identify the central message, or theme, that emerges in this excerpt of the novel. Annotate to explain the theme, and highlight evidence from the text that will help support your ideas.

## WRITING PROMPT

Squealer says, "No one believes more firmly than Comrade Napoleon that all animals are equal." Squealer also tells the animals that only Napoleon can be trusted to make the right decisions for the group. In 250 words, analyze this apparent contradiction in terms of leadership, power, and general citizen participation in government. Relate your ideas to a theme from this excerpt of the novel.

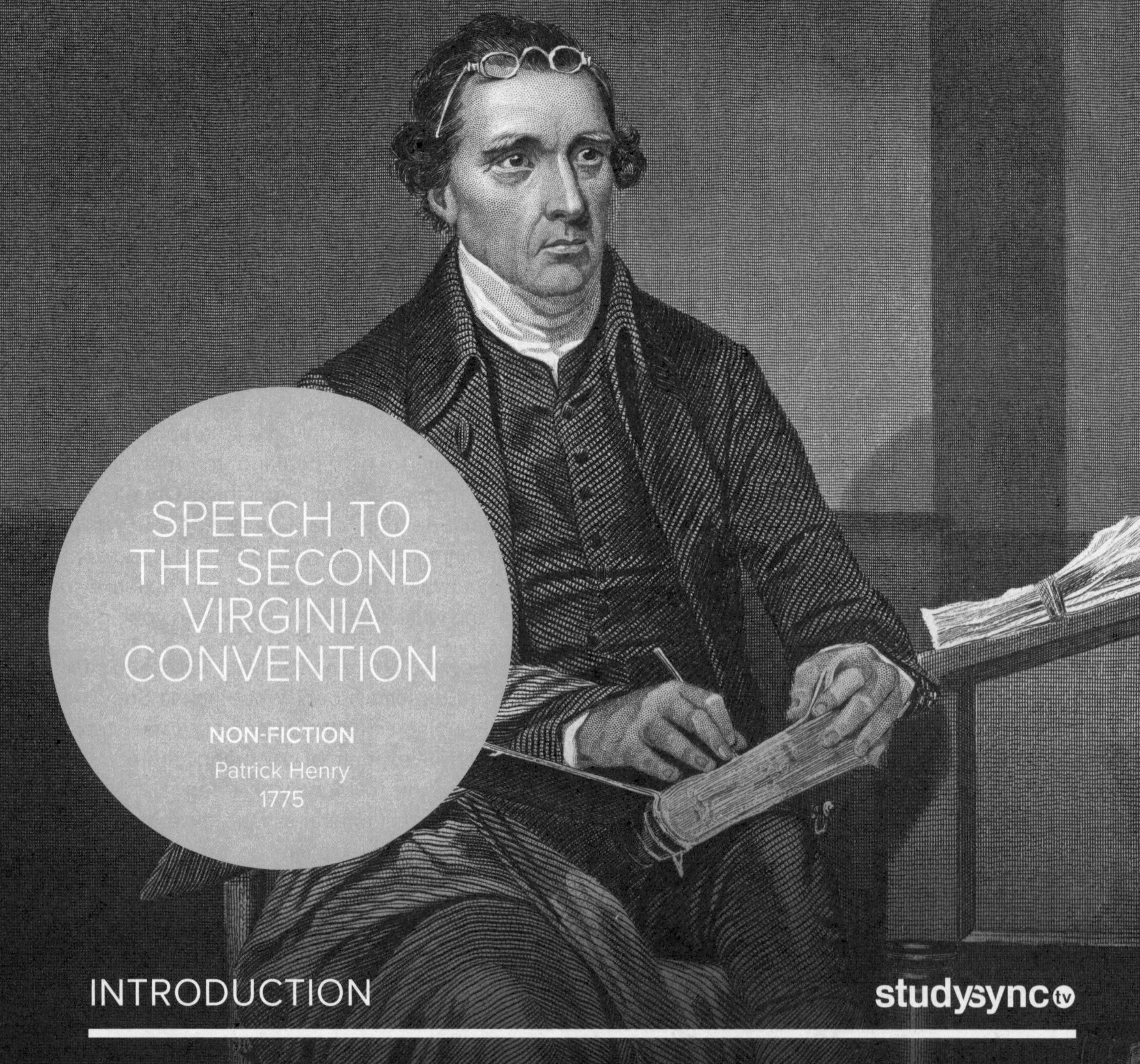

# SPEECH TO THE SECOND VIRGINIA CONVENTION

**NON-FICTION**

Patrick Henry

1775

## INTRODUCTION

studysync tv

"Different men often see the same subject in different lights," says Patrick Henry in his speech to the Second Virginia Convention, eloquently evoking reason to subtly persuade his audience. In 1775, on the eve of America's Revolutionary War, one of America's Founding Fathers, Patrick Henry, articulates his radical views with carefully constructed language intended to convince the Virginia's House of Burgesses to pass a resolution to support a war of independence against Britain. Hoping to convince Virginia to provide troops, Henry appealed to the patriotism of all those listening, including future presidents George Washington and Thomas Jefferson, with powerful oratory, including the famous line from the speech, "I know not what course others may take; but as for me, give me liberty or give me death!"

# "The war is inevitable and let it come!"

## FIRST READ

NOTES

1 Mr. President, no man thinks more highly than I do of the patriotism, as well as abilities, of the very worthy gentlemen who have just addressed the House. But different men often see the same subject in different lights; and, therefore, I hope it will not be thought disrespectful to those gentlemen if, entertaining as I do, opinions of a character very opposite to theirs, I shall speak forth my **sentiments** freely, and without reserve. This is no time for ceremony. The question before the House is one of awful moment to this country. For my own part, I consider it as nothing less than a question of freedom or slavery; and in proportion to the magnitude of the subject ought to be the freedom of the debate. It is only in this way that we can hope to arrive at truth, and fulfill the great responsibility which we hold to God and our country. Should I keep back my opinions at such a time, through fear of giving offence, I should consider myself as guilty of treason towards my country, and of an act of disloyalty toward the majesty of heaven, which I **revere** above all earthly kings.

2 Mr. President, it is natural to man to indulge in the illusions of hope. We are apt to shut our eyes against a painful truth, and listen to the song of that siren till she transforms us into beasts. Is this the part of wise men, engaged in a great and **arduous** struggle for liberty? Are we disposed to be of the number of those who, having eyes, see not, and, having ears, hear not, the things which so nearly concern their temporal salvation? For my part, whatever anguish of spirit it may cost, I am willing to know the whole truth; to know the worst, and to provide for it.

3 I have but one lamp by which my feet are guided; and that is the lamp of experience. I know of no way of judging of the future but by the past. And judging by the past, I wish to know what there has been in the conduct of the British ministry for the last ten years, to justify those hopes with which gentlemen have been pleased to solace themselves, and the House? Is it that insidious smile with which our petition has been lately received? Trust it

not, sir; it will prove a snare to your feet. Suffer not yourselves to be betrayed with a kiss. Ask yourselves how this gracious reception of our petition comports with these war-like preparations which cover our waters and darken our land. Are fleets and armies necessary to a work of love and reconciliation? Have we shown ourselves so unwilling to be reconciled, that force must be called in to win back our love? Let us not deceive ourselves, sir. These are the implements of war and **subjugation;** the last arguments to which kings resort. I ask, gentlemen, sir, what means this martial array, if its purpose be not to force us to submission? Can gentlemen assign any other possible motive for it?

4 Has Great Britain any enemy, in this quarter of the world, to call for all this accumulation of navies and armies? No, sir, she has none. They are meant for us; they can be meant for no other. They are sent over to bind and rivet upon us those chains which the British ministry have been so long forging. And what have we to oppose to them? Shall we try argument? Sir, we have been trying that for the last ten years. Have we anything new to offer upon the subject? Nothing. We have held the subject up in every light of which it is capable; but it has been all in vain. Shall we resort to entreaty and humble **supplication?** What terms shall we find which have not been already exhausted? Let us not, I beseech you, sir, deceive ourselves. Sir, we have done everything that could be done, to avert the storm which is now coming on. We have petitioned; we have remonstrated; we have supplicated; we have prostrated ourselves before the throne, and have implored its interposition to arrest the tyrannical hands of the ministry and Parliament. Our petitions have been slighted; our remonstrances have produced additional violence and insult; our supplications have been disregarded; and we have been spurned, with contempt, from the foot of the throne. In vain, after these things, may we indulge the fond hope of peace and reconciliation. There is no longer any room for hope. If we wish to be free, if we mean to preserve inviolate those inestimable privileges for which we have been so long contending, if we mean not basely to abandon the noble struggle in which we have been so long engaged, and which we have pledged ourselves never to abandon until the glorious object of our contest shall be obtained, we must fight! I repeat it, sir, we must fight! An appeal to arms and to the God of Hosts is all that is left us!

5 They tell us, sir, that we are weak; unable to cope with so formidable an adversary. But when shall we be stronger? Will it be the next week, or the next year? Will it be when we are totally disarmed, and when a British guard shall be stationed in every house? Shall we gather strength by irresolution and inaction? Shall we acquire the means of effectual resistance, by lying supinely on our backs, and hugging the delusive phantom of hope, until our enemies shall have bound us hand and foot? Sir, we are not weak if we make a proper use of those means which the God of nature hath placed in our

power. Three millions of people, armed in the holy cause of liberty, and in such a country as that which we possess, are invincible by any force which our enemy can send against us. Besides, sir, we shall not fight our battles alone. There is a just God who presides over the destinies of nations; and who will raise up friends to fight our battles for us. The battle, sir, is not to the strong alone; it is to the vigilant, the active, the brave. Besides, sir, we have no election. If we were base enough to desire it, it is now too late to retire from the contest. There is no retreat but in submission and slavery! Our chains are forged! Their clanking may be heard on the plains of Boston! The war is inevitable and let it come! I repeat it, sir, let it come. It is in vain, sir, to extenuate the matter. Gentlemen may cry, Peace, Peace but there is no peace. The war is actually begun! The next gale that sweeps from the north will bring to our ears the clash of resounding arms! Our brethren are already in the field! Why stand we here idle? What is it that gentlemen wish? What would they have? Is life so dear, or peace so sweet, as to be purchased at the price of chains and slavery? Forbid it, Almighty God! I know not what course others may take; but as for me, give me liberty or give me death!

## THINK QUESTIONS

CA-CCSS: CA.RI.9-10.1, CA.RI.9-10.4, CA.L.9-10.4a, CA.L.9-10.4b

1. Who is Patrick Henry's audience for the speech? What passage from the speech helps you answer? Support your answer with textual evidence.

2. Explain how Patrick Henry alerts his listeners to the urgency of his message. What actions being taken by the British in 1775 require an immediate response from the colonists, according to Henry? Support your answer with textual evidence.

3. The purpose of Henry's speech is to persuade his audience to take action. What specific action does Henry urge his audience to take? Provide textual evidence for your response. Why do you think the precise purpose of Henry's speech only becomes clear in the second half of the speech rather than the first?

4. Use context to identify a more familiar synonym of the word **sentiments,** which appears in the first paragraph of the speech. Explain how this synonym in the same sentence helps you determine the meaning of the word **sentiments.**

5. Use context to identify a word that seems to be related to the word **subjugation,** which appears in the third paragraph of the speech. Explain how this related word in the next sentence, along with your knowledge of the prefix "*sub-*" which means "under or beneath," help you determine the meaning of the word **subjugation.**

# CLOSE READ

CA-CCSS: CA.RI.9-10.1, CA.RI.9-10.6, CA.W.9-10.1a, CA.W.9-10.1b, CA.W.9-10.4, CA.W.9-10.6, CA.W.9-10.9b, CA.W.9-10.10

Reread the excerpt from "Speech to the Second Virginia Convention." As you reread, complete the Focus Questions below. Then use your answers and annotations from the questions to help you complete the Writing Prompt.

## FOCUS QUESTIONS

1. What point of view does Henry convey in the second paragraph of the speech and to what purpose? Highlight and annotate evidence to support your analysis.
2. The delegates at the Second Virginia Convention, Patrick Henry's audience, were largely in favor of diplomatic resolution. How does Henry further his purpose by addressing the concerns of those who wonder if another course of action besides war might be available? Highlight and annotate specific text evidence from the fourth paragraph to support your response.
3. The British believed and many delegates feared that the colonists were too weak to take on the British. What is Henry's point of view on this point? What tactics does he use to persuade his audience to share his point of view? Highlight and annotate specific text evidence from the fifth paragraph to support your response.
4. What does Henry believe will happen if the colonists fail to act now against the British? Highlight and annotate emotional appeals and language Henry uses in the final lines of his speech to build momentum and accomplish his purpose of rousing his audience to immediate action.
5. Based on details presented throughout the speech, when does Patrick Henry believe it is not only appropriate but necessary to challenge authority? Reread the text in its entirety and then highlight and annotate revealing details within the text.

## WRITING PROMPT

Suppose that you were one of the other delegates present at the Second Virginia Convention. Write a 300-word speech you might give in response to Patrick Henry, either to support or refute his argument about preparing for war with the British. Use textual evidence to evaluate how effectively Henry conveyed his point of view and achieved his purpose. Your speech, like Henry's, should convey a clear point of view; support that point of view with details and examples; make logical as well as emotional appeals; and use rhetorical techniques such as figurative language, allusions, and rhetorical questions to convey your perspective and support your purpose of either supporting or refuting Henry's argument. Perhaps you might even coin a line worthy of going down in the history books alongside Henry's "Give me liberty or give me death!"

# THE BALLAD OF BIRMINGHAM

**POETRY**

Dudley Randall

1965

## INTRODUCTION

Dudley Randall was an African-American poet and publisher who served for a time as Poet Laureate of Detroit. "The Ballad of Birmingham" is the most well-known of his poems, many of which were written during the tumultuous period of the Civil Rights Movement. The poem, written from the point of view of a mother who has lost her child, evokes the pain and confusion caused by the 1963 Birmingham church bombing, which killed four young African

"No, baby, no, you may not go, For I fear those guns will fire."

NOTES

## FIRST READ

1 "Mother dear, may I go downtown
2 Instead of out to play,
3 And march the streets of Birmingham
4 In a Freedom March today?"

5 "No, baby, no, you may not go,
6 For the dogs are **fierce** and **wild,**
7 And clubs and hoses, guns and jails
8 Aren't good for a little child."

9 "But, mother, I won't be alone.
10 Other children will go with me,
11 And march the streets of Birmingham
12 To make our country free."

13 "No, baby, no, you may not go,
14 For I fear those guns will fire.
15 But you may go to church instead,
16 And sing in the children's choir."

17 She has combed and brushed her night-dark hair,
18 And bathed rose petal sweet,
19 And **drawn** white gloves on her small brown hands,
20 And white shoes on her feet.

21 The mother smiled to know her child
22 Was in the **sacred** place,
23 But that smile was the last smile
24 To come upon her face.

NOTES

25 For when she heard the explosion,
26 Her eyes grew wet and wild.
27 She raced through the streets of Birmingham
28 Calling for her child.

29 She **clawed** through bits of glass and brick,
30 Then lifted out a shoe.
31 "O, here's the shoe my baby wore,
32 But, baby, where are you?"

## THINK QUESTIONS CA-CCSS: CA.RL.9-10.1, CA.L.9-10.4a

1. Why does the mother in the poem deny her child the chance to join one of the Freedom Marches in downtown Birmingham? Cite evidence from the poem to support your answer.

2. Based on details in the text, describe the purpose of the Freedom Marches and who participated in them.

3. What is ironic about the mother's decision to send her child to sing in the church choir instead of to march on the streets? Explain your answer using textual evidence.

4. Use context clues from the poem to infer the meaning of the word **fierce** as it is used in the text. Write your definition of "fierce" here, and explain how you got it.

5. Use context clues to determine what the speaker means when he or she says that the mother's eyes grew **wild.** How is this meaning of "wild" different from the word's first appearance in stanza 2? How is it similar? Explain your answer.

## CLOSE READ

CA-CCSS: CA.RL.9-10.1, CA.RL.9-10.4, CA.RL.9-10.6, CA.L.9-10.5b, CA.W.9-10.4, CA.W.9-10.5, CA.W.9-10.9a, CA.W.9-10.10

Reread the poem "The Ballad of Birmingham". As you reread, complete the Focus Questions below. Then use your answers and annotations from the questions to help you complete the Writing Prompt.

### FOCUS QUESTIONS

1. In the fourth stanza, highlight words that are associated with the church and words that are associated with the street. How do the different connotations of these words set up a contrast between the church and the street that later proves to be ironic? Make annotations to support your explanation.
2. Highlight vivid descriptions and words with strong connotations in the fifth stanza, lines 17-20. Use the annotation tool to explain how these words emphasize the child's purity and innocence.
3. What are the connotations of the word *clawed* in the eighth and last stanza? How is this connotation similar to that of the word *wild* in the seventh stanza, and how does each serve to convey the mother's state of mind?
4. Highlight other words in the eighth and last stanza that help create strong mental images for readers. What effect are such images likely intended to have and why? Explain your answer using the annotation tool.
5. Based on details in the text, what might have been the poet's purpose in writing this piece? What point of view might he have had toward the Civil Rights Movement and the costs of taking a stand?

### WRITING PROMPT

Dudley Randall wrote "The Ballad of Birmingham" after the real-life bombing that occurred in 1963 in Birmingham, Alabama, during the period of the Civil Rights Movement. Research details about the bombing and its historical context. Then use your research findings to analyze how the poem includes both facts from the historical record about actual events that took place in Birmingham, Alabama as well as literary dramatizations of these events. Which details can be confirmed by source materials? How does the fictionalized material enhance the description of the real-life events and their impact on readers? Finally, explain how the poet's word choices in the poem, and the connotations of many of those words, may suggest Randall's point of view and message about the protests, the bombing, and the impact of the violence on families. How does his choice of words differ from those used in the factual accounts you found? Be sure to include specific examples from the text as well as information obtained from research to support your analysis.

# REMARKS TO THE SENATE IN SUPPORT OF A DECLARATION OF CONSCIENCE

**NON-FICTION**

Margaret Chase Smith

1950

## INTRODUCTION

studysync tv

Margaret Chase Smith, a Republican from Maine, was the first woman to serve in both the House of Representatives and the Senate. In this famous speech, delivered four months after Senator Joseph McCarthy made his inflammatory claim that the State Department was "infested" with Communists, beginning a dark period in Congressional history, Smith reaches out to her colleagues and calls for a return to civility and responsibility.

# "As an American, I want to see our nation recapture the strength and unity it once had..."

## FIRST READ

Mr. President:

1 I would like to speak briefly and simply about a serious national condition. It is a national feeling of fear and frustration that could result in national suicide and the end of everything that we Americans hold dear. It is a condition that comes from the lack of effective leadership in either the Legislative Branch or the Executive Branch of our Government.

2 That leadership is so lacking that serious and responsible proposals are being made that national advisory commissions be appointed to provide such critically needed leadership.

3 I speak as briefly as possible because too much harm has already been done with irresponsible words of bitterness and selfish political **opportunism**. I speak as briefly as possible because the issue is too great to be obscured by eloquence. I speak simply and briefly in the hope that my words will be taken to heart.

4 I speak as a Republican. I speak as a woman. I speak as a United States Senator. I speak as an American.

5 The United States Senate has long enjoyed worldwide respect as the greatest deliberative body in the world. But recently that deliberative character has too often been **debased** to the level of a forum of hate and character assassination sheltered by the shield of congressional immunity.

6 It is ironical that we Senators can in debate in the Senate directly or indirectly, by any form of words, **impute** to any American who is not a Senator any conduct or motive unworthy or unbecoming an American—and without that non-Senator American having any legal redress against us—yet if we say the same thing in the Senate about our colleagues we can be stopped on the grounds of being out of order.

NOTES

7 It is strange that we can verbally attack anyone else without restraint and with full protection and yet we hold ourselves above the same type of criticism here on the Senate Floor. Surely the United States Senate is big enough to take self-criticism and self-appraisal. Surely we should be able to take the same kind of character attacks that we "dish out" to outsiders.

8 I think that it is high time for the United States Senate and its members to do some soul-searching—for us to weigh our consciences—on the manner in which we are performing our duty to the people of America—on the manner in which we are using or abusing our individual powers and privileges.

9 I think that it is high time that we remembered that we have sworn to uphold and defend the Constitution. I think that it is high time that we remembered that the Constitution, as amended, speaks not only of the freedom of speech but also of trial by jury instead of trial by accusation.

10 Whether it be a criminal prosecution in court or a character prosecution in the Senate, there is little practical distinction when the life of a person has been ruined.

11 Those of us who shout the loudest about Americanism in making character assassinations are all too frequently those who, by our own words and acts, ignore some of the basic principles of Americanism:

12 The right to criticize;
The right to hold unpopular beliefs;
The right to protest;
The right of independent thought.

13 The exercise of these rights should not cost one single American citizen his reputation or his right to a livelihood nor should he be in danger of losing his reputation or livelihood merely because he happens to know someone who holds unpopular beliefs. Who of us doesn't? Otherwise none of us could call our souls our own. Otherwise thought control would have set in.

14 The American people are sick and tired of being afraid to speak their minds lest they be politically smeared as "Communists" or "Fascists" by their opponents. Freedom of speech is not what it used to be in America. It has been so abused by some that it is not exercised by others.

15 The American people are sick and tired of seeing innocent people smeared and guilty people whitewashed. But there have been enough proved cases, such as the Amerasia case, the Hiss case, the Coplon case, the Gold case, to cause the nationwide distrust and strong suspicion that there may be something to the unproved, sensational accusations.

16 As a Republican, I say to my colleagues on this side of the aisle that the Republican Party faces a challenge today that is not unlike the challenge that it faced back in Lincoln's day. The Republican Party so successfully met that challenge that it emerged from the Civil War as the champion of a united nation -- in addition to being a Party that unrelentingly fought loose spending and loose programs.

17 Today our country is being psychologically divided by the confusion and the suspicions that are bred in the United States Senate to spread like cancerous tentacles of "know nothing, suspect everything" attitudes. Today we have a Democratic Administration that has developed a mania for loose spending and loose programs. History is repeating itself—and the Republican Party again has the opportunity to emerge as the champion of unity and prudence.

18 The record of the present Democratic Administration has provided us with sufficient campaign issues without the necessity of resorting to political smears. America is rapidly losing its position as leader of the world simply because the Democratic Administration has pitifully failed to provide effective leadership.

19 The Democratic Administration has completely confused the American people by its daily contradictory grave warnings and optimistic assurances—that show the people that our Democratic Administration has no idea of where it is going.

20 The Democratic Administration has greatly lost the confidence of the American people by its **complacency** to the threat of communism here at home and the leak of vital secrets to Russia though key officials of the Democratic Administration. There are enough proved cases to make this point without diluting our criticism with unproved charges.

21 Surely these are sufficient reasons to make it clear to the American people that it is time for a change and that a Republican victory is necessary to the security of this country. Surely it is clear that this nation will continue to suffer as long as it is governed by the present ineffective Democratic Administration.

22 Yet to displace it with a Republican regime embracing a philosophy that lacks political integrity or intellectual honesty would prove equally disastrous to this nation. The nation sorely needs a Republican victory. But I don't want to see the Republican Party ride to political victory on the Four Horsemen of Calumny—Fear, Ignorance, Bigotry, and Smear.

23 I doubt if the Republican Party could—simply because I don't believe the American people will uphold any political party that puts political exploitation above national interest. Surely we Republicans aren't that desperate for victory.

24 I don't want to see the Republican Party win that way. While it might be a fleeting victory for the Republican Party, it would be a more lasting defeat for the American people. Surely it would ultimately be suicide for the Republican Party and the two-party system that has protected our American liberties from the dictatorship of a one party system.

25 As members of the Minority Party, we do not have the primary authority to formulate the policy of our Government. But we do have the responsibility of rendering constructive criticism, of clarifying issues, of allaying fears by acting as responsible citizens.

26 As a woman, I wonder how the mothers, wives, sisters, and daughters feel about the way in which members of their families have been politically mangled in the Senate debate -- and I use the word "debate" advisedly.

27 As a United States Senator, I am not proud of the way in which the Senate has been made a publicity platform for irresponsible **sensationalism**. I am not proud of the reckless abandon in which unproved charges have been hurled from this side of the aisle. I am not proud of the obviously staged, undignified countercharges that have been attempted in retaliation from the other side of the aisle.

28 I don't like the way the Senate has been made a rendezvous for vilification, for selfish political gain at the sacrifice of individual reputations and national unity. I am not proud of the way we smear outsiders from the Floor of the Senate and hide behind the cloak of congressional immunity and still place ourselves beyond criticism on the Floor of the Senate.

29 As an American, I am shocked at the way Republicans and Democrats alike are playing directly into the Communist design of "confuse, divide, and conquer." As an American, I don't want a Democratic Administration "whitewash" or "cover-up" any more than I want a Republican smear or witch hunt.

30 As an American, I condemn a Republican "Fascist" just as much I condemn a Democratic "Communist." I condemn a Democrat "Fascist" just as much as I condemn a Republican "Communist." They are equally dangerous to you and me and to our country. As an American, I want to see our nation recapture the strength and unity it once had when we fought the enemy instead of ourselves.

31 It is with these thoughts that I have drafted what I call a "Declaration of Conscience." I am gratified that Senator Tobey, Senator Aiken, Senator Morse, Senator Ives, Senator Thye, and Senator Hendrickson have concurred in that declaration and have authorized me to announce their concurrence.

## THINK QUESTIONS CA-CCSS: CA.RI.9-10.1, CA.L.9-10.4a, CA.L.9-10.4b

1. Why is Senator Margaret Chase Smith addressing the U.S. Senate? To whom are the remarks delivered? Cite textual evidence to support your answer.

2. What, to Senator Smith, are the significant characteristics of the Republican Party and the Democratic Administration at the time she is delivering this speech? Why is she concerned about both of them? Cite textual evidence to support your answer.

3. Why do you think Chase Smith waits until Paragraph 14 to use the word "Communists" in her remarks? Cite textual evidence to explain your inference.

4. Use context to determine the meaning of the word **debased** as it is used in *Remarks to the Senate in Support of a Declaration of Conscience.* Write your definition here.

5. Use your understanding of word parts and the context clues provided in the passage to determine the meaning of **sensationalism.** Explain how you figured out the meaning and write your definition here.

# CLOSE READ

CA-CCSS: CA.RI.9-10.1, CA.RI.9-10.5, CA.RI.9-10.6, CA.RI.9-10.8, CA.RI.9-10.9, CA.W.9-10.1a, CA.W.9-10.1b, CA.W.9-10.4, CA.W.9-10.5, CA.W.9-10.6, CA.W.9-10.9b, CA.W.9-10.10

Reread the text from "Remarks to the Senate in Support of a Declaration of Conscience." As you reread, complete the Focus Questions below. Then use your answers and annotations from the questions to help you complete the Writing Prompt.

## FOCUS QUESTIONS

1. How does Smith contrast the rights of Senators with the rights of ordinary citizens? Highlight textual evidence in paragraphs 6-7 to support your ideas. Annotate to explain the contrasts.

2. Highlight textual evidence in paragraphs 15 and 20 that Smith gives to support the idea that Americans may have some reason to suspect their fellow citizens. Analyze the reasons and evidence she uses. Then analyze how Smith's ideas or claims are developed and refined by particular sentences or paragraphs in the text. Write annotations to explain how she supports her claims.

3. In paragraph 4, Smith makes it clear that she is speaking from a variety of points of view, all of which have joined together to express a single opinion. Highlight the text in which she identifies these points of view. Annotate to explain the value in identifying these points of view.

4. Like Patrick Henry in his *Speech to the Second Virginia Convention,* Smith speaks to what she sees as an immediate and dangerous issue and challenges her colleagues to take a new course of action. Highlight some phrases she uses to convince the other Senators of the importance of the issue. Write annotations to explain how her rhetoric compares to that of Patrick Henry, including how they address related themes and concepts in these U.S. historical documents and how their use of language helps to make their speeches effective.

5. In this speech, Smith's use of rhetoric challenges her fellow Senators over what she perceives as an abuse of power. What words and phrases help to justify her criticism? Highlight textual evidence in the first five paragraphs of the speech that help clarify Smith's reasons for issuing the challenge. Then use the annotation tool to explain your choices.

## WRITING PROMPT

If you could make a speech on an issue, what issue would it be? Taking a cue from Margaret Chase Smith, write your own Declaration of Conscience. Identify an issue of national or global importance, and write a persuasive speech for an audience of your classmates. Be sure to state your claims clearly and to support them with sound reasons and relevant textual evidence. Make your purpose for writing and your point of view clear, and remember that your speech is to persuade your audience to agree with your point of view about the issue. Once you have finished writing, review Smith's speech. Write a brief explanation of how your speeches are alike, yet different.

# TEXAS V. JOHNSON

**NON-FICTION**

U.S. Supreme Court
1989

## INTRODUCTION

In 1989, the U.S. Supreme Court ruled that states could not prohibit citizens from desecrating the flag as a form of protest, determining that such an act constitutes protected speech under the First Amendment. This excerpt from the Court's ruling summarizes the case and provides passages from both the majority and the

# "The American flag played a central role in our Nation's most tragic conflict..."

## FIRST READ

TEXAS v. JOHNSON
Argued March 21, 1989
Decided June 21, 1989

1 During the 1984 Republican National Convention in Dallas, Texas, respondent Johnson participated in a political **demonstration** to protest the policies of the Reagan administration and some Dallas-based corporations. After a march through the city streets, Johnson burned an American flag while protesters chanted. No one was physically injured or threatened with injury, although several witnesses were seriously offended by the flag burning. Johnson was convicted of desecration of a venerated object in violation of a Texas statute, and a State Court of Appeals affirmed. However, the Texas Court of Criminal Appeals reversed, holding that the State, consistent with the First Amendment, could not punish Johnson for burning the flag in these circumstances. The court first found that Johnson's burning of the flag was **expressive** conduct protected by the First Amendment. The court concluded that the State could not criminally sanction flag desecration in order to preserve the flag as a symbol of national unity. It also held that the statute did not meet the State's goal of preventing breaches of the peace, since it was not drawn narrowly enough to encompass only those flag burnings that would likely result in a serious disturbance, and since the flag burning in this case did not threaten such a reaction. Further, it stressed that another Texas statute prohibited breaches of the peace and could be used to prevent disturbances without punishing this flag desecration.

2 Held:

3 Johnson's conviction for flag desecration is inconsistent with the First Amendment.

...

NOTES

4 JUSTICE BRENNAN delivered the opinion of the Court.

...

5 We are tempted to say, in fact, that the flag's deservedly cherished place in our community will be strengthened, not weakened, by our holding today. Our decision is a reaffirmation of the principles of freedom and inclusiveness that the flag best reflects, and of the conviction that our toleration of criticism such as Johnson's is a sign and source of our strength. Indeed, one of the proudest images of our flag, the one immortalized in our own national anthem, is of the bombardment it survived at Fort McHenry. It is the Nation's resilience, not its rigidity, that Texas sees reflected in the flag - and it is that resilience that we reassert today.

6 The way to preserve the flag's special role is not to punish those who feel differently about these matters. It is to persuade them that they are wrong. "To courageous, self-reliant men, with confidence in the power of free and fearless reasoning applied through the processes of popular government, no danger flowing from speech can be deemed clear and present, unless the incidence of the evil apprehended is so imminent that it may befall before there is opportunity for full discussion. If there be time to expose through discussion the falsehood and **fallacies,** to avert the evil by the processes of education, the remedy to be applied is more speech, not enforced silence." And, precisely because it is our flag that is involved, one's response to the flag burner may exploit the uniquely persuasive power of the flag itself. We can imagine no more appropriate response to burning a flag than waving one's own, no better way to counter a flag burner's message than by saluting the flag that burns, no surer means of preserving the dignity even of the flag that burned than by- as one witness here did - according its remains a respectful burial. We do not consecrate the flag by punishing its desecration, for in doing so we dilute the freedom that this cherished emblem represents.

...

7 CHIEF JUSTICE REHNQUIST, with whom JUSTICE WHITE and JUSTICE O'CONNOR join, dissenting.

8 For more than 200 years, the American flag has occupied a unique position as the symbol of our Nation, a uniqueness that justifies a governmental **prohibition** against flag burning in the way respondent Johnson did here.

9 At the time of the American Revolution, the flag served to unify the Thirteen Colonies at home, while obtaining recognition of national sovereignty abroad.

...

NOTES

10 The American flag played a central role in our Nation's most tragic conflict, when the North fought against the South. The lowering of the American flag at Fort Sumter was viewed as the start of the war. . . .

11 In the First and Second World Wars, thousands of our countrymen died on foreign soil fighting for the American cause. At Iwo Jima in the Second World War, United States Marines fought hand to hand against thousands of Japanese. By the time the Marines reached the top of Mount Suribachi, they raised a piece of pipe upright and from one end fluttered a flag. That ascent had cost nearly 6,000 American lives. . . .

12 Both Congress and the States have enacted numerous laws regulating misuse of the American flag. Until 1967, Congress left the regulation of misuse of the flag up to the States. Now, however, 18 U.S.C. 700(a) provides that:

13 "Whoever knowingly casts contempt upon any flag of the United States by publicly mutilating, defacing, defiling, burning, or trampling upon it shall be fined not more than $1,000 or imprisoned for not more than one year, or both."

• • •

14 The American flag, then, throughout more than 200 years of our history, has come to be the visible symbol embodying our Nation. It does not represent the views of any particular political party, and it does not represent any particular political philosophy. The flag is not simply another "idea" or "point of view" competing for recognition in the marketplace of ideas. Millions and millions of Americans regard it with an almost mystical **reverence** regardless of what sort of social, political, or philosophical beliefs they may have. I cannot agree that the First Amendment invalidates the Act of Congress, and the laws of 48 of the 50 States, which make criminal the public burning of the flag.

## THINK QUESTIONS CA-CCSS: CA.RI.9-10.1, CA.L.9-10.4a, CA.L.9-10.4d, CA.L.9-10.4c

1. What legal issue is this Supreme Court case about? What are the two points of view? Cite textual evidence to support your answer.

2. What ruling did the Supreme Court make in the Texas v. Johnson case? Write two or three sentences explaining Justice Brennan's majority opinion on this legal issue. Cite textual evidence that includes two or three reasons for the Court's decision.

3. Write three or four sentences explaining the dissenting point of view as expressed by Chief Justice Rehnquist and two other justices in the minority opinion. In what ways do these justices disagree with Justice Brennan? Cite textual evidence to support your answer.

4. Use context to determine the meaning of the word **fallacies** as it is used in *Supreme Court Ruling: Texas v. Johnson, 1989*. Write your definition of *fallacies,* as it is used in paragraph 5, and explain how you determined the meaning of the word. Verify your meaning by looking up the word in a print or digital dictionary.

5. Use the context of Chief Justice Rehnquist's opinion about the history of the American flag to determine the meaning of **reverence,** as it is used in paragraph 13 of *Supreme Court Ruling: Texas v. Johnson, 1989.* Write your definition of *reverence* and explain how you determined the meaning. Then consult a general or specialized reference material, such as a print or digital college-level dictionary to determine the precise meaning of the word.

# CLOSE READ

CA-CCSS: CA.RI.9-10.1, CA.RI.9-10.2, CA.RI.9-10.4, CA.RI.9-10.5, CA.RI.9-10.6, CA.RI.9-10.8, CA.RI.9-10.9, CA.L.9-10.6, CA.W.9-10.1a, CA.W.9-10.1b, CA.W.9-10.1d, CA.W.9-10.1e, CA.W.9-10.4, CA.W.9-10.5, CA.W.9-10.6, CA.W.9-10.9b, CA.W.9-10.10

Reread the *Supreme Court Ruling: Texas versus Johnson, 1989*. As you reread, complete the Focus Questions below. Then use your answers and annotations from the questions to help you complete the Writing Prompt.

## FOCUS QUESTIONS

1. As you reread the first section of *Supreme Court Ruling: Texas v. Johnson, 1989*, analyze how the author unfolds a description of the events and how connections are made between the events. How and why did the Supreme Court conclude that Johnson's burning of the flag is protected by the First Amendment? Highlight textual evidence in the text. Use the annotation tool to define technical language, as needed, and to explain how the author explains the outcome of the case.

2. Reread Chief Justice Rehnquist's dissent from the majority opinion. What is the central idea of his disagreement with the court's majority opinion, as stated by Justice Brennan? What arguments does Rehnquist use to support his disagreement? Highlight textual evidence, including technical language, and annotate to explain your ideas.

3. How does the technical language of the legal system affect the meaning and tone of this text? What technical language does Justice Brennan use to show how the reactions to the flag burning influence the applications of law to this case? Highlight your evidence and make annotations to explain your choices.

4. Compare and contrast the points of view of the two justices when it comes to the challenge of deciding the rules on flag burning. On what points do the justices agree? On what points do they disagree? Highlight evidence from the text that will help support your opinion, and write annotations to explain your understanding of their reasoning.

5. Reread Justice Brennan's decision. Analyze in detail how Brennan's ideas or claims are developed. What claim does he make about the value of the court's decision? Which key details support this claim? How does he support Johnson's challenge of the rules? Highlight evidence, including technical language, to support your ideas and write annotations to explain your choices.

## WRITING PROMPT

You have read two opposing points of view in the landmark decision titled *Supreme Court Ruling: Texas v. Johnson, 1989.* In your opinion, do you agree or disagree with the Supreme Court's ruling? To decide, think about which justice made the stronger argument about whether or not flag burning is an "expressive conduct" protected by freedom of speech under the First Amendment? Do you agree with Justice Brennan, who delivered the Supreme Court ruling and overturned Mr. Johnson's conviction? Or do you agree with Chief Justice Rehnquist, who wrote the minority, or dissenting, opinion upholding Johnson's conviction for flag burning? Write an argumentative essay about which judge's argument you found more convincing. State your claim clearly and support it with arguments, using strong reasons, technical language, and evidence from the text. Be sure to state the claim and counterclaim of the two justices. Use a formal style and an objective tone in your writing, and provide a conclusion that follows from and supports the argument you presented. Use appropriate technical language to support the legal points you make.

# IMPASSIONED ARGUMENTS MARK HIGH COURT FLAG-BURNING DECISION

**NON-FICTION**

Judy Weissler
1989

## INTRODUCTION

This newspaper article originally appeared in the *Houston Chronicle* on June 22, 1989. The article summarizes the U.S. Supreme Court decision on the Texas v. Johnson flag-burning case, which determined that Gregory Lee Johnson's conviction for burning the U.S. flag at a protest in Dallas was inconsistent

"Johnson soaked the flag in kerosene and set it afire."

NOTES

## FIRST READ

1 WASHINGTON—The Supreme Court's **fragmented** affirmation of First Amendment rights in a Texas flag-burning case was marked by impassioned **rhetoric** rom both the majority and the **dissent.**

2 The court split 5–4 in its decision, for the first time deciding the government may not impose criminal penalties to punish such activity as long as it is peaceful.

3 "We do not consecrate the flag by punishing its desecration, for in doing so we dilute the freedom that this cherished emblem represents," Justice William Brennan wrote for the court. He was joined in the opinion by Justices Thurgood Marshall, Harry Blackmun, Antonin Scalia and Anthony Kennedy.

4 But Chief Justice William Rehnquist—in a dissent notable for its extensive quotations of poetry and song—said the First Amendment should not be interpreted to **invalidate** laws passed by Congress and by 48 of the 50 states prohibiting the burning of the flag.

5 "The government may conscript men into the armed forces where they must fight and perhaps die for the flag, but the government (under the new ruling) may not prohibit the public burning of the banner under which they fight," Rehnquist wrote. The other dissenting justices were Byron White, Sandra O'Connor and John Paul Stevens.

6 The court's opinion wipes out the conviction of former Houston resident Gregory Lee (Joey) Johnson, a member of the Revolutionary Communist Youth Brigade who was sentenced to a year in jail and fined $2,000 for burning a flag in downtown Dallas during the 1984 Republican National Convention.

NOTES

7 The Texas Court of Criminal Appeals reversed the conviction, on **grounds** that the Texas law was overbroad and inconsistent with the First Amendment guarantees of free speech. The Supreme Court affirmed the lower court's ruling.

8 Texas officials had argued that the state law prohibiting desecration of the flag is justified as a way to preserve a symbol of national unity and to prevent breaches of the peace.

9 But Brennan said the flag will be an even stronger symbol of freedom under the new court finding, he said, and there was never any real threat of breach of the peace from Johnson's symbolic act.

10 "The First Amendment literally forbids the abridgement only of 'speech,' but we have long recognized that its protection does not end at the spoken or written word," Brennan wrote.

11 "If there is a bedrock principle underlying the First Amendment, it is that the government may not prohibit the expression of an idea simply because society finds the idea itself offensive or disagreeable . . . We have not recognized an exception to this principle even where our flag has been involved."

12 Johnson, who said he lived in Houston for four years following the flag-burning incident, said his case was "an important victory . . . but I refuse to attribute this to the Supreme Court, the Constitution, to justice having prevailed . . . because this is the same Supreme Court and the same Constitution that's being used to carry out vicious and oppressive decisions against all the civil rights cases of the 1960s."

13 Johnson said he is "looking forward to coming back" to Houston. "I'm going to be politically preparing the ground for revolution there . . . I don't know at this point when that's going to happen."

14 The Dallas prosecutors who used the state law to convict Johnson continued to insist that flag-burning is not protected by the First Amendment.

15 "Texas had sought to punish Mr. Johnson for his destruction of the flag, not for any ideas he sought to convey by the act. We agree with Justice Stevens that sanctioning the public destruction of the flag may tarnish its value for all Americans," Dallas Assistant District Attorney Kathi A. Drew said in a written statement.

16 Alan Slobodin, attorney for the conservative Washington Legal Foundation, said the decision is "outrageous" and "offensive to deeply held views about the flag and respect for the flag and people who've died for the flag.

The court is apparently going to give carte blanche to a bunch of extremist groups."

17 The Texas law used to prosecute Johnson made it a criminal offense to "intentionally or knowingly desecrate . . . a state or national flag . . . in a way the actor knows will seriously offend one or more persons likely to observe or discover his actions."

18 Johnson was among a group of protesters outside Dallas City Hall on Aug. 22, 1984. They staged "die-ins" by collapsing on the ground in a symbol of nuclear war and spray-painted buildings and tore up potted plants and papers.

19 The flag-burning occurred when about 50 people formed a circle and chanted, "America, the red, white and blue—we spit on you."

20 Johnson soaked the flag in kerosene and set it afire.

21 Brennan wrote that Johnson was prosecuted not because his actions might cause a breach of the peace—since there was no violence associated with the demonstration—but because his expression could offend others.

22 But Rehnquist invoked the 200-year history of the nation to show that the flag has "a uniqueness" in the nation that justifies a governmental prohibition against flag burning.

23 He quoted passages about the flag from Ralph Waldo Emerson's *Concord Hymn,* from the *Star Spangled Banner* and extensively from the poem Barbara Frietchie by John Greenleaf Whittier, which includes the famous lines:

24 Shoot if you must
This old grey head
But spare your country's flag.

---

## THINK QUESTIONS

CA-CCSS: CA.RI.9-10.1, CA.L.9-10.4a

1. How does the first sentence, or lead, of the article effectively introduce the content to come as well as capture readers' attention and interest? Cite textual evidence to support your answer.

2. Identify both practical and emotional arguments Rehnquist used as the basis for his dissent against the court's decision. Cite textual evidence to support your answer.

3. Explain Justice Brennan's view of Johnson's prosecution. Why did Brennan believe the prosecution was unjust? Use evidence from the passage to support your ideas and any inferences you make.

4. Use context to determine the meaning of the word **invalidate.** Explain how clues in the article helped you arrive at this meaning.

5. Use context to determine the meaning of the word **fragmented** as it is used in the article. Explain how clues in the article helped you arrive at this meaning.

## CLOSE READ

CA-CCSS: CA.RI.9-10.1, CA.RI.9-10.2, CA.RI.9-10.3, CA.RI.9-10.4, CA.RI.9-10.7, CA.L.9-10.5b, CA.W.9-10.1a, CA.W.9-10.1b, CA.W.9-10.4, CA.W.9-10.5, CA.W.9-10.6, CA.W.9-10.9b, CA.W.9-10.10

Reread the text from "Impassioned Arguments Mark High Court Flag Burning Decision." As you reread, complete the Focus Questions below. Then use your answers and annotations from the questions to help you complete the Writing Prompt.

### FOCUS QUESTIONS

1. Compare and contrast the opening of the newspaper article with the opening of the court decision excerpt. How does the writer of the article use language to "tell a story" rather than list facts about a topic? Consider in your analysis the writer's use of the word "fragmented." What connotations does this word have and how does it impact the opening of the article? How might a word with a similar denotation but different connotation change the tone? Highlight evidence and annotate to support your ideas.

2. What is the purpose of the sixth and seventh paragraphs in the article? How do they enhance readers' understanding of the Supreme Court's decision, the most important point explored in the article? Highlight evidence and annotate to support your ideas.

3. How would you describe the way the writer organizes the information in this newspaper article? Are the paragraphs long or short? Why? Highlight evidence in paragraphs 8 through 11 to support your ideas and annotate to explain your choices.

4. Reread the final three paragraphs of the article. What effect is this section likely to have on readers? Why might the writer have chosen to end the article with Rehnquist's quotation? Highlight evidence and annotate to support your ideas.

5. How does the Supreme Court's decision about flag-burning shed legal light on the question of when it is appropriate to challenge the rules? Highlight evidence and annotate to support your ideas.

### WRITING PROMPT

In a 300-word analysis, compare and contrast the newspaper article "Impassioned Arguments Mark High Court Flag-Burning Decision" with the library excerpt of the court opinion *Texas v. Johnson*. Identify similarities and differences in the information both selections include, their organizational structure, and the kind of language the authors employ. Offer reasons why differences might exist and speculate about what effects they might have on readers. Why might a reader exploring this landmark case about the flag and its use in acts of symbolic protest benefit from experiencing both texts? Cite specific evidence from both texts to support your analysis.

## INTRODUCTION

In these two articles the writers make arguments for and against the rights of American citizens to burn the country's flag as a form of political protest. This debate has been going on since American activist Gregory Lee Johnson was arrested in Dallas, Texas, for burning the American flag outside of the Republican National Convention in 1984. Both writers present strong arguments and support their claims with evidence. Which one does the better job convincing you that his or her view is correct?

# "All citizens must understand that the right to burn the flag is protected by America's Constitution."

## FIRST READ

**Burning the American Flag: First Amendment Right or a Crime?**

**Point**: The Right to Burn the Flag Is Protected by Freedom of Speech

1 When a citizen of a nation is dissatisfied with the government, what can he or she do to try to create change? What if voting in elections and participating in local government doesn't seem to be enough? This is exactly the position some citizens find themselves in when they make the choice to burn the flag as a form of protest. Many see it as a last resort. All citizens must understand that the right to burn the flag is protected by America's Constitution.

2 There are many people who do not support the legal right to burn the flag. They feel that burning the flag is **callous** toward the military servicemen and women who have fought and died for their country. Anyone can see how this act would be hurtful toward members of the armed forces. However, it is not **plausible** to say that in order to protect freedom, you must limit the very freedoms you are trying to protect. Even some service members agree. According to a veteran of the Vietnam War, Richard Savage, "... Those who would burn the flag destroy the symbol of freedom, but amending the Constitution would destroy part of freedom itself."

3 The United States Supreme Court agrees that it would be unethical to limit citizens' personal freedoms with laws against burning the flag. In 1984, Gregory Lee Johnson burned the American flag at the Republican National Convention in Dallas because he was dissatisfied with the government of the United States. At the time it was illegal in the state of Texas to burn the flag, so Johnson was arrested. Johnson fought the case and it went all the way to the Supreme Court. The Court ruled in 1989 that burning a flag is symbolically the same as exercising your right to free speech, and therefore it is protected by the First Amendment to the Constitution. Since the Constitution is the

NOTES

supreme law of the land, states are no longer allowed to make or enforce laws against burning the flag.

4 Citizens like Gregory Lee Johnson who make the decision to burn the American flag in protest probably do not take the decision lightly. Instead, they are weighing their reverence for the flag carefully with their civic duty to stand up for what they believe in. One of the most important patriotic ideals in the United States is that the government is for the people and by the people. By burning a flag in protest, a citizen is participating in politics and therefore fulfilling his or her civic duty. It is far more unpatriotic to either not act to try to improve the government, or to use inadequate methods to try to bring about change.

5 To those who say flag burning should be illegal despite this evidence, I have a few questions. What exactly would be protected by a law that makes it illegal to burn flags? Clothing featuring American flags? Fourth of July picnic napkins and plates? Although it sounds a bit absurd, this is not very far-fetched. According to the Federal Flag Code, which was signed by President Franklin Roosevelt in 1942, a flag is anything "by which the average person seeing the same without deliberation may believe the same to represent the flag." A law against burning flags could have the negative, unintended consequence of unnecessary litigation against people that harm an image of the flag with no intention of protest.

6 The Supreme Court got this one right. When someone burns the flag in protest they are exercising their right to free speech, and that is a freedom that should never be tarnished by the government. The men and women who decide to burn the flag in protest would not bother to take action if they were not devoted to the betterment of the United States.

**Counterpoint:** Burning the American Flag Is a Threat to Our Country

7 The American flag is one of the most sacred symbols of the United States. When six Marines raised the American flag over Iwo Jima in 1945, it symbolized the United States' strength in the face of world powers that wanted to destroy us. Three of the Marines that raised that flag would make the ultimate sacrifice for their country when they were killed in action. When Neil Armstrong placed an American Flag on the moon in 1969, it was a symbol of the United States' resolve to be a leader in science and technology despite competition from the repressive Communist regimes. When New York City firefighters raised the flag over the ruins of the World Trade Center in 2001, it was a symbol of solidarity and strength after an **atrocious** attack on the American people. To burn the United States flag for any reason is disrespectful and should be outlawed.

8 Unfortunately, there are some people who think it is acceptable to burn this sacred symbol as a form of protest against the government. They mistakenly believe that it is **feasible** to fight for freedom while simultaneously destroying one if its most cherished symbols. On the contrary, burning the American flag is deeply disrespectful to those that actually fight for freedom: members of the armed forces. Anyone that thinks that it should be legal to burn the flag should consider the following points of view.

9 Think how it must feel to be an American service member injured in battle. You are happy to be alive but you have a long road to recovery. Then you come home to the injurious act of the same citizens you fought to protect, burning a symbol of the freedom you fought for. Now picture tears in the eyes of the child or spouse of a soldier that went missing in action while fighting for our country. Imagine how it must feel for them to see people disrespecting a symbol of the freedom their missing loved one fought for, not knowing if their family member will ever have their own freedom again. Consider a serviceman or woman that fought in battle and made it home, but carries the memory of his or her comrades that were not so lucky to make it back to their families alive. How would it feel to see the memory of their fallen comrades degraded by the burning of the flag?

10 People who think it should be legal to burn the American flag argue that the Supreme Court ruled it is a right protected by the Constitution. However, this is not a sufficient reason to let the issue lie. The Supreme Court has been wrong before. There was a time when the Supreme Court ruled that African Americans could not be American citizens (Dred Scott v. Sandford, 1857). Then only a little more than ten years later the Thirteenth, Fourteenth, and Fifteenth Amendments to the Constitution were passed, reversing this decision and ensuring that all Americans enjoy the protection of the law. One of the wonderful things about the United States is that the Constitution is flexible, and it is **imperative** that it be adjusted to reflect respect for the American flag as well.

11 In fact, the majority of Americans think that it should be illegal to burn the flag. In a poll conducted in 1990, 69% of Americans said that they supported a Constitutional Amendment that would make it legal for Congress or individual states to pass laws against flag burning. Since the United States government is for the people and by the people, public opinion should matter in deciding this issue.

12 And perhaps the most compelling reason to make burning the American flag illegal, is that it is a threat to national security. Simply put, when American citizens burn the flag it makes us look weak to our enemies. The world we live in today is increasingly threatening. It is essential that the United States show a united and strong nation that will not tolerate aggression from others.

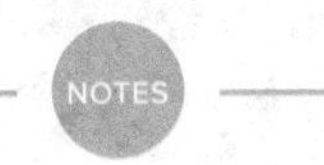


13 Internationally there is a precedent for limiting freedom of expression in the interest of national security. The European Convention on Human Rights is an international treaty that has been in place in Europe since 1953. Article 10 (the section on freedom of expression) of the ECHR states: "The exercise of these freedoms, since it carries with it duties and responsibilities, may be subject to such formalities, conditions, restrictions or penalties as are prescribed by law and are necessary in a democratic society, in the interests of national security, territorial integrity or public safety...."

14 The clear message here is that it is more important to protect our citizens than to allow such an extreme display of freedom of speech. If you are dissatisfied with the government, there are many options available to you. Go out and vote. Speak or write about your point of view in a public forum so that your message can be heard. Run for office. Any of these would be better than the disrespectful, depraved act of burning the most sacred symbol of the freedoms you enjoy.

## THINK QUESTIONS CA-CCSS: CA.RI.9-10.1, CA.L.9-10.4a, CA.L.9-10.4d

1. For what reasons does the author of the "Point" essay support the right to burn the flag as a protest? Support your answer with both ideas that are directly stated and ideas that you have inferred from textual evidence.

2. For what reasons does the author of the "Counterpoint" essay oppose giving people the right to burn the flag as a protest? Support your answer with both ideas that are directly stated and ideas that you have inferred from clues in the text.

3. Use the reading-comprehension technique of asking and answering questions to compare the two essays. How do the authors appeal to the readers? What kind of evidence do the authors use to back up their opinions? Support your answer with evidence from the text.

4. Use context to determine the meaning of the word **callous** as it is used in the "Point" essay. Write your definition of **callous** here and explain how you determined it. Then check your inferred meaning in a print or digital dictionary.

5. Based on context clues and the knowledge that the Latin suffix "*-ible*" means "able to," determine the meaning of the word **feasible** as it is used in the "Counterpoint" essay. Write your definition of *feasible* here and explain how you determined it.

## CLOSE READ

CA-CCSS: CA.RI.9-10.1, CA.RI.9-10.6, CA.RI.9-10.8, CA.W.9-10.4, CA.W.9-10.5, CA.W.9-10.6, CA.W.9-10.9b, CA.W.9-10.10

Reread the text "Burning the Flag." As you reread, complete the Focus Questions below. Then use your answers and annotations from the questions to help you complete the Writing Prompt.

### FOCUS QUESTIONS

1. In paragraph 4, in the "Point" essay, the author claims that "By burning a flag in protest, a citizen is participating in politics and therefore fulfilling his or her civic duty. It is far more unpatriotic to either not act to try to improve the government, or to use inadequate methods to try to bring about change." How does the author support this claim? Explain why you think his argument is reasonable or fallacious. Highlight text evidence to support your evaluation. Use the annotation tool to explain your thinking.

2. In paragraph 9, in the "Counterpoint" essay, the author argues that the flag is a symbol of freedom and that burning the flag causes emotional distress to many Americans, especially members of the armed forces and their families. Does the author provide relevant evidence for this argument? How does rhetoric affect the argument? Highlight evidence in the text that you would consider relevant. Then use the annotation tool to explain why this evidence does or does not convince you that flag burning as protest should be banned.

3. In paragraph 12, in the "Counterpoint" essay, the author claims that flag burning is a threat to our national security. Evaluate the reasons and evidence that the author supplies. Are the reasons faulty or reasonable? Is there sufficient and relevant evidence for the author's argument? Highlight evidence from the text and annotate to support your evaluation.

4. Paragraph 13, in the "Counterpoint" essay, presents a precedent for limiting freedom of expression in the interest of national security. The author concludes that: "The clear message here is that it is more important to protect our citizens than to allow such an extreme display of freedom of speech." Explain why you think this is a reasonable or a fallacious argument. What does the author mean by "extreme display of freedom of speech?" What makes it extreme or not extreme? Highlight evidence from the text and annotate to support your explanation.

5. Read the following excerpt from paragraph 10, in the "Counterpoint" essay, and think about the importance of both setting and being able to challenge the rules. Does the author provide convincing arguments for amending the Constitution to prohibit flag burning? Why or why not? Highlight textual evidence and annotate to explain and support your answers.

   People who think it should be legal to burn the American flag argue that the Supreme Court ruled it is a right protected by the Constitution. However, this is not a sufficient reason to let the issue lie. The Supreme Court has been wrong before. There was a time when the Supreme Court ruled that African Americans could not be American citizens (Dred Scott v. Sandford, 1857). Then only a little more than ten years later the Thirteenth, Fourteenth, and Fifteenth Amendments to the Constitution were passed, reversing this decision and ensuring that all Americans enjoy the protection of the law.

6. People who think it should be legal to burn the American flag argue that the Supreme Court ruled it is a right protected by the Constitution. However, this is not a sufficient reason to let the issue lie. The Supreme Court has been wrong before. There was a time when the Supreme Court ruled that African Americans could not be American citizens (Dred Scott v. Sandford, 1857). Then only a little more than ten years later the Thirteenth, Fourteenth, and Fifteenth Amendments to the Constitution were passed, reversing this decision and ensuring that all Americans enjoy the protection of the law.

7. The author of the "Point" essay believes that flag burning is an appropriate way to challenge the rules. What claim does the author make about flag burning and citizenship? How does this claim support the idea that flag burning is an appropriate way to challenge the rules? Highlight text evidence to support your evaluation. Use the annotation tool to explain your thinking.

## WRITING PROMPT

Imagine that, like a constitutional law attorney, you have an opportunity to argue for or against a law or rule. Write an argument concerning a law or rule that you are familiar with and have an opinion about. You can use an actual rule, law, or legal decision or a plausible one that you create. Clearly state the rule, law, or legal decision and use your understanding of valid reasons and evidence to support your argument. Use the appropriate rhetoric to explain your reasoning. Anticipate fallacious or faulty reasoning from the other side of the argument, and address it. Provide relevant and sufficient evidence for your argument.

# THE PEASANT REVOLT

English Language Development

NON-FICTION

## INTRODUCTION

Many hardships and burdens had been placed on the French peasants in the late 1700s. How did they respond? What did they do to show their discontent?

# "Suddenly mass hysteria, fed by wild rumors, spread across rural France."

## FIRST READ

NOTES

1 The population of France at the beginning of the eighteenth century was more than twenty million people. The majority, about eighty percent, was concentrated in rural areas, villages, and very small cities.

2 People who owned bits of land and people who worked in the countryside were known as peasants. There were many levels of peasants, which differed dramatically in status and wealth. Peasants who were in the best position rented land to others and lived off the profits. On the opposite end were desperate day workers looking only for enough food and a place to rest. In the middle were independent farmers, renters, and sharecroppers. No matter the level, in years with poor harvests, ninety percent of the peasants barely had enough to feed their families.

3 Another group living in the countryside was the nobles and non-nobles who owned **extravagant** manor houses. They lived off the work of the peasants. The stark contrast between the peasant group and the nobles and non-nobles group was one of the factors leading to the French Revolution.

4 Year after year the peasants had grown poorer. Any drought resulted in catastrophe and famine. Peasants had no voice in government. They **endured** hardships and endless inequalities, such as burdensome taxes. Not only were they required to pay a land tax and a poll tax to the State, but the lord of the manor also demanded rents and contributions, and the clergy collected tithes, or a percentage of income and harvest. The government, deeply in debt, also taxed items such as salt, which was essential for food preservation. About ten to twenty thousand men, women, and children in each province became beggars. Furthermore, peasants were the only class that could be forced into military service. Understandably, the peasants felt intense anger and resentment against those who **suppressed** them and endangered their families.

5 Then the riots began. On July 14, 1789, the citizens of Paris, terrified that troops of King Louis XVI might attack them, **stormed** the Bastille, a fortress in the city. More than 100 people died. People in the countryside heard the news, and rumors spread like wildfire. The peasants, hearing of the capture of the Bastille, decided that social change just might be possible. A small flame of hope was ignited.

6 Peasants also heard stories of troops gathering with the approval of King Louis XVI. The troops would be sent to the countryside to kill peasants and stop any rebellions. Then something called the "Great Fear" mobilized the countryside and destroyed many lives.

7 Suddenly mass hysteria, fed by wild rumors, spread across rural France. Peasants believed in an "aristocratic conspiracy." That is, frightened nobles would hire armed men, or "brigands," to burn crops, steal food, and attack the villages in order to stop rebellion. The peasants were confused and terrorized. They feared that their homes would be burned and they would lose what little they had. Misinformation flowed across the countryside like water after a heavy storm. No one bothered to verify the rumors. They all seemed possible and probably true. The natural reaction was to strike first.

8 Peasants formed armed groups to defend their fields and their homes, but defense was not enough. Driven by fear, terrified peasants began attacking manors. They burned grain, looted manors, and leveled walls that separated them from the lord. They even stole weather vanes, which to them symbolized the wealth of the manor. Most important of all, they found and destroyed **deeds** that dictated the dues peasants had to pay the lord.

9 Targeting the manor houses was a logical response to the built-up hatred of the aristocracy. Peasants loathed paying the dues demanded by the lord. They no longer wanted to live on the edge of potential starvation. They despised the class system that made them the lowest of the low. They wanted the manor system destroyed.

10 George Lefebvre, noted French historian, commented that the uprising in Paris and the threat of brigands were magnified because it was harvest time. No one had any doubt that the aristocrats were paying the brigands. Was that a fact? Probably not, but the rebellion continued and eventually ended the reign of the monarchy in France.

## USING LANGUAGE

CA-CCSS: ELD.PI.9-10.6.c.Ex

Review the prefix and suffix guide below. Use the guide to help you with the activity. Complete the chart by writing the correct new word to the third column from the options, and then writing the definition of that word in the fourth column. The first one is done for you.

| Prefix or Suffix | Meaning |
|---|---|
| *micro-* | small |
| *non-* | no |
| *-ly* | in the manner of |
| *-less* | without |
| *dis-* | not, away, apart |

| New Word Options |
|---|
| rapidly |
| nonprofit |
| disorganized |
| blameless |
| microorganism |

| Prefix/Suffix | Root Word | New Word | Word Definition |
|---|---|---|---|
| *micro-* | organism | microorganism | a small organism |
| *non-* | profit | | |
| *-ly* | rapid | | |
| *-less* | blame | | |
| *dis-* | organized | | |

## MEANINGFUL INTERACTIONS CA-CCSS: ELD.PI.9-10.7.Ex

How well does the writer use a cause-and-effect text structure to help the reader understand the lives of peasants in France? Focus your discussion on paragraph 4. Review the text that is boldfaced. You can use the speaking frames below to help express your ideas in the discussion. Then, use the self-assessment rubric to evaluate your participation in the discussion.

4 Year after year the peasants had grown poorer. Any drought resulted in catastrophe and famine. Peasants had no voice in government. They endured hardships and endless inequalities, such as burdensome taxes. Not only were they required to pay a land tax and a poll tax to the State, but the lord of the manor also demanded rents and contributions, and the clergy collected tithes, or a percentage of income and harvest. The government, deeply in debt, also taxed items such as salt, which was essential for food preservation. About ten to twenty thousand men, women, and children in each province became beggars. Furthermore, peasants were the only class that could be forced into military service. **Understandably, the peasants felt intense anger and resentment against those who suppressed them and endangered their families.**

- I think the word/phrase/sentence . . . effectively creates a cause-and-effect relationship within the text because . . .
- The word/phrase/sentence . . . suggests . . .
- The word/phrase/sentence . . . helps to explain that the effect was the French Revolution because . . .
- Another sentence in the paragraph that could be identified as another cause for the revolution is . . .

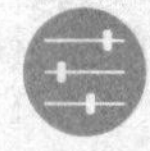

## SELF-ASSESSMENT RUBRIC CA-CCSS: ELD.PI.9-10.6.a.Ex, ELD.PI.9-10.7.Ex

| | 4<br>I did this well. | 3<br>I did this pretty well. | 2<br>I did this a little bit. | 1<br>I did not do this. |
|---|---|---|---|---|
| I expressed my ideas clearly. | | | | |
| I supported my ideas using evidence from the text. | | | | |
| I clearly explained cause and effect relationships in the text. | | | | |
| I worked with my partner to analyze how the structure helps readers understand the text. | | | | |

## REREAD

Reread paragraphs 1–5 of "The Peasant Revolt." After you reread, complete the Using Language and Meaningful Interactions activities.

## USING LANGUAGE CA-CCSS: ELD.PII.9-10.4.Ex

Fill in each blank to create an expandable noun phrase for each sentence.

1. **Write an expanded noun phrase for "houses" in the following sentence.**

   Peasants were unable to afford ______________________________ houses.

2. **Write an expanded noun phrase for "taxes" in the following sentence.**

   ______________________________ taxes placed immense pressure on the peasants.

3. **Write an expanded noun phrase for "storm" in the following sentence.**

   The French Revolution swept the country like a ______________________________ storm.

4. **Write an expanded noun phrase for "groups" in the following sentence.**

   ______________________________ groups defended fields and homes.

## MEANINGFUL INTERACTIONS CA-CCSS: ELD.PI.9-10.1.Ex

How well does the writer use language to show that the poor conditions of the peasants helped to bring about social change? Focus your discussion on paragraph 2. Review the text that is boldfaced. You can use the speaking frames below to help express your ideas in the discussion. Remember to follow turn-taking rules during the discussion and affirm other's opinions. Then, use the self-assessment rubric to evaluate your participation in the discussion.

2 People who owned bits of land and people who worked in the countryside were known as peasants. There were many levels of peasants, which differed dramatically in status and wealth. Peasants who were in the best position rented land to others and lived off the profits. **On the opposite end were desperate day workers looking only for enough food and a place to rest.** In the middle were independent farmers, renters, and sharecroppers. **No matter the level, in years with poor harvests, ninety percent of the peasants barely had enough to feed their families.**

- I think the word/phrase/sentence . . . effectively creates a sense that peasants lived in poor conditions because . . .
- The word/phrase/sentence . . . suggests . . .
- I agree with . . . because . . .
- I like your point that . . . because . . . , but I think . . .

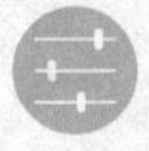

## SELF-ASSESSMENT RUBRIC CA-CCSS: ELD.PI.9-10.1.Ex

| | 4<br>I did this well. | 3<br>I did this pretty well. | 2<br>I did this a little bit. | 1<br>I did not do this. |
|---|---|---|---|---|
| I expressed my ideas clearly. | | | | |
| I supported my ideas using evidence from the text. | | | | |
| I helped to affirm other's opinions. | | | | |
| I took turns sharing my ideas with the group. | | | | |

# REREAD

Reread paragraphs 6–10 of "The Peasant Revolt." After you reread, complete the Using Language and Meaningful Interactions activities.

## USING LANGUAGE CA-CCSS: ELD.PII.9-10.3.Ex

Fill in each blank to complete the sentences.

1. **Write the present tense of "believe" to complete the sentence.**

   Peasants ______________________ in an "aristocratic conspiracy."

2. **Write the future tense of "sent" to complete the sentence.**

   The troops ______________________ to the countryside to kill peasants and stop any rebellions.

3. **Write the past tense of "end" to complete the sentence.**

   The rebellion continued and eventually ______________________ the reign of the monarchy in France.

4. **Write the past tense of "want" to complete the sentence.**

   They no longer ______________________ to live on the edge of potential starvation.

5. **Write the future tense of "revolt" to complete the sentence.**

   The peasants ______________________ to overtake the government.

6. **Write the past tense of "burn" to complete the sentence.**

   They ________________ grain, looted manors, and leveled walls that separated them from the lord.

7. **Write the future tense of "find" to complete the sentence.**

   They ____________________ and destroying deeds that dictated the dues peasants had to pay the lord.

## MEANINGFUL INTERACTIONS

**CA-CCSS:** ELD.PI.9-10.6.a.Ex, ELD.PI.9-10.6.b.Ex

What is the author's point of view in paragraphs 6–10? What evidence from the text supports your conclusion? You can use the speaking frames below to help express your ideas in the discussion.

- I think the author's point of view is . . .
- Evidence that supports my idea is . . .
- The word/phrase/sentence . . . suggests . . .
- I agree/disagree with . . . because . . .

# THE DINNER OF THE LION

English Language Development

**FICTION**

## INTRODUCTION

A lion demands honor and respect from animals who are destined to be his dinner. Will they bow before him and be eaten? Or will one of them come up with a solution to this big, furry problem?

"Life was marvelous for the animals in the Seven Hills, until the lion moved in."

## FIRST READ

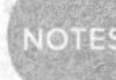


1 The water was pure, and the grass was green. Life was marvelous for the animals in the Seven Hills, until the lion moved in. He believed he was the smartest, the strongest, and the most beautiful of all animals. His long, yellow mane rippled in the breeze like a flag announcing his greatness.

2 Lion believed he could do whatever he liked. He liked making others afraid. He insisted on being called "His Lordship." Even worse, he devoured two or three animals every day, creating great **dread** among them all. They became so frightened that they could hardly eat. This infuriated His Lordship because the quality of his meals slowly **diminished.** In the best of times he could be called extremely unpleasant. These were not the best of times. His Lordship roared in fury, and the sound echoed in the hills like nearby thunder.

3 The animals, quaking in fear, held a meeting. It would be easier to please the lion if only one animal were eaten a day. Then more might survive to see their children grow up. Weasel was sent to negotiate with His Lordship.

4 "Your honor," he began, "we fear for your health because the quality of your meals is poor. We suggest that, instead of you hunting down two or three of us, we will bring you one plump and extremely tender animal every day. You won't have to waste your time hunting. You are too great for such nonsense."

5 His Lordship, soaking up **flattery** like a sponge, agreed with an added threat. "My meal must arrive on time. Bring it with the honor that is due me. I am great and deserve respect! If you disappoint me, I will eat all of you in a single day." Weasel retired from His Lordship's presence, bowing in obedience.

6 When Weasel reported back to the animals, they were torn between two feelings. It was better that only one of them got eaten every day, but if His Lordship was not happy, they would all die. Only Hare saw the faulty **logic.**

7 "If he ate all of us," Hare explained, "there would be no more food, so he would die, too. He simply enjoys threatening others with extreme, but unlikely **measures."**

8 However, the animals were not sure about that at all, and so they lived in fear of angering His Lordship. Each day they drew a name from a bowl to see who would be on the day's menu. Each animal worried, thinking, "Tomorrow it may be my turn, and I will never see my children again."

9 Everyone worried except Hare. When it was his turn, he seemed as tranquil as a summer breeze. He told the others, "I have a plan."

10 Hare dashed to the river and jumped in. Then he rolled around on the riverbank until his whole body except for his head was covered with disgusting, smelly mud. Satisfied, Hare strolled toward His Lordship's den. He began to run when he was about one hundred feet away. Appearing out of breath, he threw himself at His Lordship's feet.

11 "How dare you present me with a dirty meal!" His Lordship bellowed.

12 "Forgive me, oh great His Lordship who is the Greatest," Hare panted, "I am not the dinner. Another lion stole the delicious hare I was bringing you! The lion was bigger and stronger than you. His yellow mane blew so beautifully in the breeze."

13 His Lordship screamed in fury. "I am the GREATEST! No other lion is allowed in these hills! Show me that evil lion, and I will destroy him!"

14 Hare led the way to the old well. "He took your dinner and jumped in," Hare said, pretending to be frightened.

15 His Lordship looked into the well, and Hare peered over the edge at the same time. They saw the reflections of a lion and a neat, clean hare's head. "I will smash you, I will shatter you, because I am the Great Lion who owns these hills!" shrieked His Lordship. With that he hurled himself into the well and was never seen again.

16 The animals had quite a pleasant party that evening, and Hare lived to see his children, his grandchildren, and even his great grandchildren grow up.

## USING LANGUAGE

CA-CCSS: ELD.PI.9-10.6.c.Ex

Read each sentence. Choose the correct definition for the boldfaced multiple-meaning word. Use a dictionary if needed.

1. "Your honor," he began, "we fear for your health because the quality of your meals is **poor**."
   - O inferior in quality
   - O having little or no money

2. You are too **great** for such nonsense."
   - O large in size
   - O superior in quality

3. We will bring a plump and **tender** animal each day.
   - O loving and gentle
   - O easily chewed

4. Weasel **retired** from Lion's presence.
   - O moved away
   - O stopped working

5. Weasel **reported** what had happened.
   - O complained about
   - O gave an account of

6. Bring it with the **honor** that is due me.
   - O a privilege
   - O high respect

7. "If you disappoint me, I will eat all of you in a **single** day."
   - O only one
   - O not married

8. It was a **breeze** to put the plan in action.
   - O easy to do
   - O gentle wind

## MEANINGFUL INTERACTIONS CA-CCSS: ELD.PI.9-10.1.Ex

What problems and solutions shape the plot of the story? Focus your discussion on paragraphs 3, 6, and 15. Review the text that is boldfaced. You can use the speaking frames below to help express your ideas in the discussion. Remember that your discussion should be supported by asking relevant, on-topic questions and providing on-topic and well-supported answers. Then, use the self-assessment rubric to evaluate your participation in the discussion.

3 The animals, quaking in fear, held a meeting. **It would be easier to please the lion if only one animal were eaten a day. Then more might survive to see their children grow up.** Weasel was sent to negotiate with His Lordship.

6 When Weasel reported back to the animals, they had mixed feelings. **It was better that only one of them got eaten every day, but if His Lordship was not happy, they would all die.** Only Hare saw the faulty logic.

15 His Lordship looked into the well, and Hare peered over the edge at the same time. **They saw the reflections of a lion and a neat, clean hare's head. "I will smash you, I will shatter you, because I am the Great Lion who owns these hills!" shrieked His Lordship.** With that he hurled himself into the well and was never seen again.

- The main problem is . . .
- This problem may be hard to solve because . . .
- One possible solution the animals come up with is . . .
- I do/don't think this is a good solution because . . .
- The animals worry this solution has created another problem because . . .
- Hare's plan is to . . .
- I think this solution works well because . . .

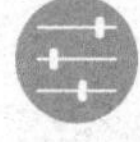

## SELF-ASSESSMENT RUBRIC CA-CCSS: ELD.PI.9-10.1.Ex

| | 4<br>I did this well. | 3<br>I did this pretty well. | 2<br>I did this a little bit. | 1<br>I did not do this. |
|---|---|---|---|---|
| I expressed my ideas clearly. | | | | |
| I supported my ideas using evidence from the text. | | | | |
| I explained what problems and solutions shape the plot of the story. | | | | |
| I asked only relevant, on-topic questions during the discussion. | | | | |

# REREAD

Reread paragraphs 1–9 of "The Dinner of the Lion." After you reread, complete the Using Language and Meaningful Interactions activities.

## USING LANGUAGE CA-CCSS: ELD.PI.9-10.6.c.Ex

Read each passage. Examine the figurative language that appears in boldface as well as any context clues that point to its meaning. Then choose the correct answer to the question found beneath the passage.

1. His Lordship roared in fury, and the **sound echoed in the hills like nearby thunder**. The animals, quaking in fear, held a meeting.

   Based on the figurative language, what word best describes the sound of His Lordship's roar?

   ○ loud
   ○ clear

2. "You are too great for such nonsense." His Lordship, **soaking up flattery like a sponge**, agreed, adding a threat...

   What does the figurative phrase "soaking up flattery like a sponge" tell us about His Lordship?

   ○ He didn't care about compliments.
   ○ He liked what he heard.

3. Everyone worried except Hare. When it was his [Hare's] turn, he seemed **as tranquil as a summer breeze**.

   Based on the figurative language, what is another word to describe Hare?

   ○ calm
   ○ refreshing

4. When Weasel reported back to the animals, they were **torn between two feelings**. It was better that only one of them got eaten every day, but if His Lordship was not happy, they would all die.

   Based on the figurative phrase "torn between two feelings," how do the animals feel about Weasel's report?

   ○ unsure
   ○ hurt

## MEANINGFUL INTERACTIONS

CA-CCSS: ELD.PI.9-10.1.Ex, ELD.PI.9-10.6.b.Ex

What inferences can you make about the characters in "The Dinner of the Lion" based on details in the text? Focus your discussion on paragraphs 4, 5, and 7. Work with partners or small groups to practice sharing and discussing your inferences, using the speaking frames. Then, use the self-assessment rubric to evaluate your participation in the discussion. Remember to affirm the ideas of others during the discussion.

- I think that Lion is . . . because . . .
- This evidence supports the idea that . . .
- I think that Weasel is . . . because . . .
- This evidence supports the idea that . . .
- I think that Hare is . . . because . . .
- This evidence supports the idea that . . .
- I think . . . said that . . .
- I agree with . . . that . . .

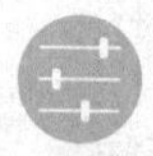

## SELF-ASSESSMENT RUBRIC

CA-CCSS: ELD.PI.9-10.1.Ex

| | 4<br>I did this well. | 3<br>I did this pretty well. | 2<br>I did this a little bit. | 1<br>I did not do this. |
|---|---|---|---|---|
| I expressed my ideas clearly. | | | | |
| I made inferences about the characters based on details in the text. | | | | |
| I supported my ideas with evidence from the text. | | | | |
| I affirmed the ideas of others in my group. | | | | |

## REREAD

Reread paragraphs 10–16 of "The Dinner of the Lion." After you reread, complete the Using Language and Meaningful Interactions activities.

## USING LANGUAGE

CA-CCSS: ELD.PI.9-10.12.b.Ex

Choose the correct word to complete each sentence.

1. Weasel was sent to ______ with Lion.
   - ○ negotiating
   - ○ negotiate
   - ○ negotiated

2. Weasel ______ a deal with Lion and reported back to the other animals.
   - ○ negotiated
   - ○ negotiates
   - ○ negotiating

3. When ______ with a Lion, it's best to pay a lot of compliments.
   - ○ negotiation
   - ○ negotiating
   - ○ negotiate

4. Weasel seems to be a good ______.
   - ○ negotiating
   - ○ negotiate
   - ○ negotiator

5. Lion considered himself to be ______.
   - ○ great
   - ○ greatly
   - ○ greater

6. Lion refused to consider that another lion could be ______ than himself.
   - ○ greatest
   - ○ greater
   - ○ great

7. Lion was ______ angered when Hare mentioned the other lion.
   - ○ great
   - ○ greatly
   - ○ greatest

8. Lion was convinced that he was the ______ in the entire land.
   - ○ greatest
   - ○ great
   - ○ greater

9. Life in the Seven Hills became very ______ after Lion arrived.
   - ○ pleasant
   - ○ unpleasant
   - ○ pleasantly

10. Hare spoke ______ despite being yelled at a number of times.
    - ○ pleasantly
    - ○ pleasant
    - ○ unpleasant

## MEANINGFUL INTERACTIONS

CA-CCSS: ELD.PI.9-10.1.Ex, ELD.PI.9-10.11.a.Ex

Which do you think played the strongest role in determining the story's outcome: Lion's pride or Hare's cleverness? What evidence from the text supports your opinion?

- My opinion is that . . . played the strongest role in determining the story's outcome. My opinion is based on . . .
- This evidence supports the idea that . . .

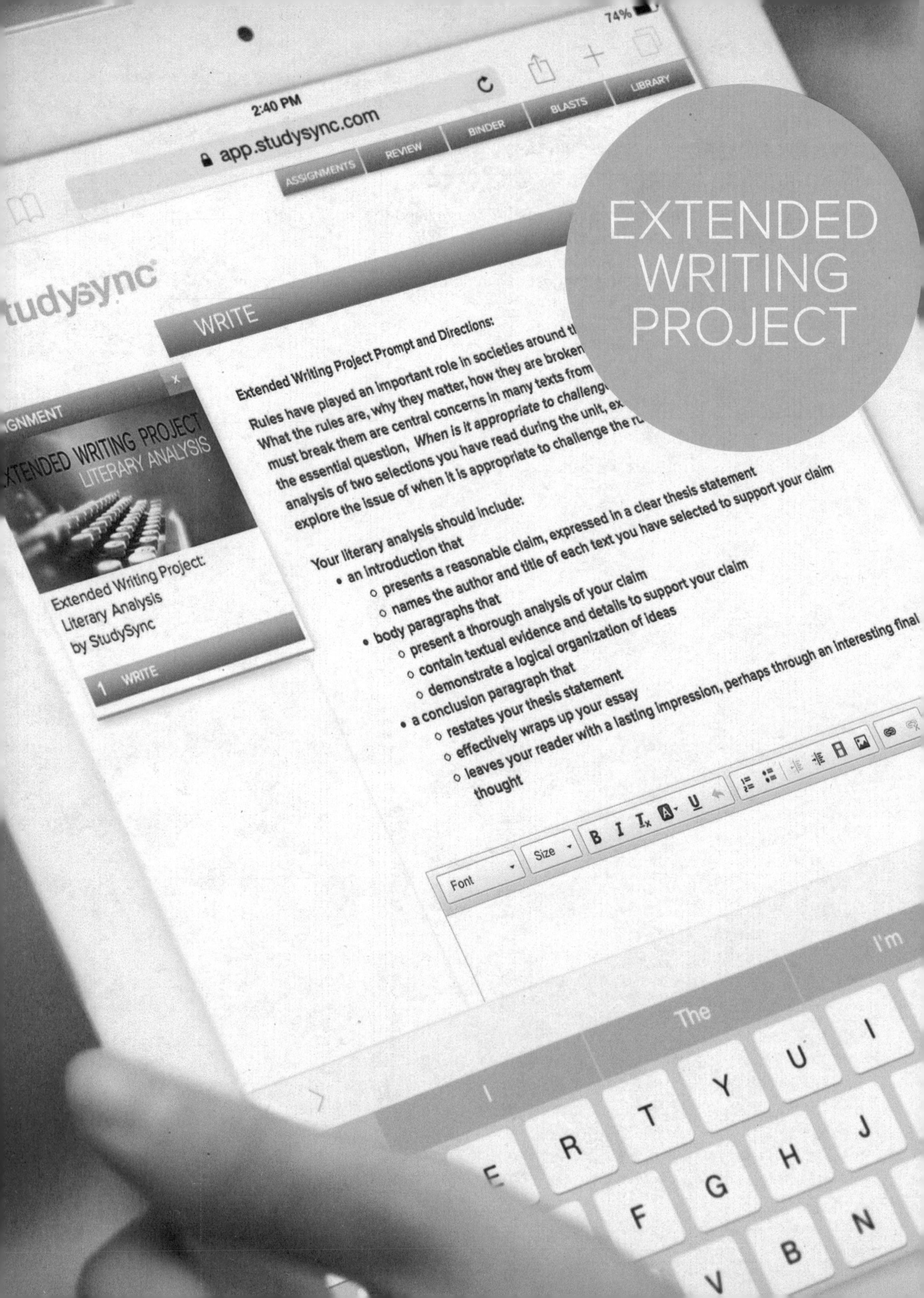
EXTENDED WRITING PROJECT
2:40 PM
74%
app.studysync.com
ASSIGNMENTS
REVIEW
BINDER
BLASTS
LIBRARY
WRITE
Extended Writing Project Prompt and Directions:
Your literary analysis should include:
an introduction that
presents a reasonable claim, expressed in a clear thesis statement
names the author and title of each text you have selected to support your claim
body paragraphs that
present a thorough analysis of your claim
contain textual evidence and details to support your claim
demonstrate a logical organization of ideas
a conclusion paragraph that
restates your thesis statement
effectively wraps up your essay
leaves your reader with a lasting impression, perhaps through an interesting final thought
Extended Writing Project:
Literary Analysis
by StudySync
WRITE
Font
Size

NOTES

# LITERARY ANALYSIS

## WRITING PROMPT

Rules have played an important role in societies around the world and across the ages. What the rules are, why they matter, how they are broken, and why some people feel they must break them are central concerns in many texts from this unit, which seeks to answer the essential question, *When is it appropriate to challenge the rules?* Write a literary analysis of two selections you have read during the unit, examining how the authors explore the issue of when it is appropriate to challenge the rules.

Your literary analysis should include:

- an introduction that
  - presents a reasonable claim, expressed in a clear thesis statement
  - names the author and title of each text you have selected to support your claim
- body paragraphs that
  - present a thorough analysis of your claim
  - contain textual evidence and details to support your claim
  - demonstrate a logical organization of ideas
- a conclusion paragraph that
  - restates your thesis statement
  - effectively wraps up your essay
  - leaves your reader with a lasting impression, perhaps through an interesting final thought

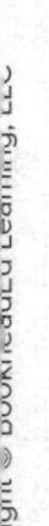

**Argumentative writing** requires a writer to make a claim or take a position on a topic and then to identify, evaluate, and provide textual evidence that offers reasonable support for the claim. Literary analysis is a form of argumentative writing. In a **literary analysis,** a writer takes a position on one or more works of literature to demonstrate why authors used particular text structures, word

choices, ideas, images, or literary devices in their work. Literary analysis is not a summary of the literature. Instead, it is an opportunity for a writer to share his or her personal perspectives, critical thinking, or interpretation of works of literature.

Strong argumentative writing, of which literary analysis is an example, begins with an introductory paragraph that provides a general context for the topic and then presents a reasonably narrow thesis statement that explicitly states the writer's position on the topic. The body paragraphs of an argumentative piece of writing, such as an essay, are focused on relevant textual details that provide evidence in support of the main idea. Argumentative essays often contain direct quotations, or citations, from the texts being analyzed. The language used must be clear, coherent, formal in tone, and appropriate to its task, purpose, and intended audience. Argumentative essays stay focused on the main idea and claim by using transition words to help create flow and make connections between supporting details and citations. Strong argumentative essays then end with a conclusion that revisits the main point of the thesis statement and synthesizes the evidence that has been provided. The features of argumentative writing include:

- an introductory paragraph with a clear thesis statement
- a clear and logical organizational structure
- supporting details, including valid reasoning and textual evidence, properly cited
- effective transitions to show the connections between ideas
- a formal style and objective tone
- a concluding paragraph that summarizes the analysis and restates the thesis

## STUDENT MODEL

You will learn skills of the writer's craft as you follow the writing process steps of Prewrite, Plan, Draft, and Revise, before the final step of Edit, Proofread, and Publish. Before you get started on your own argumentative essay, begin by reading this essay that one student wrote in response to the writing prompt. As you read this student model, highlight and annotate the features of argumentative writing that the student included in his essay.

### Breaking the Rules

*Rules are often thought of as the bricks and mortar that people use to construct the societies they live in. Rules, we are told, keep the wheels of society turning,*

NOTES

provide people with basic necessities, keep peace and order, and secure the well-being of citizens. Without rules, nations and whole cultures would likely descend into chaos and eventual self-destruction. Yet rules can be perverted and used to violate the needs and rights of the people they are meant to serve. Sophocles's play *Antigone* and George Orwell's novel *Animal Farm* provide examples of events and situations in which it is clear that sometimes rules may rightly be challenged and broken, although not without consequences.

In the opening scene of *Antigone,* Sophocles introduces the audience to the initial conflict of the play: whether or not to obey King Creon's decree. Antigone and Ismene's brothers—Polyneices and Eteocles—have killed each other during battle. Eteocles, who fought on the side of the victorious city of Thebes, has been buried with the full rituals of a Greek citizen and soldier. However, Creon, the new king of Thebes, has ordered that Polyneices, who fought against Thebes, should remain unburied. His body is to remain on the open battlefield, and his spirit is condemned to roam the land without peace. Antigone has asked to meet her sister outside the gates of Thebes to plea for help in taking Polyneices' body for proper burial. Should Antigone break the law or not? This is the problem Sophocles explores.

Immediately, the two sisters begin to argue over the whether or not Creon's decree should be followed. As the sisters show their differences, the audience gets a chance to see both sides of the argument. Ismene believes that it is the role of Greek citizens, especially women, to follow the rules set down by the male leaders of their society. Ismene warns, "Shall we not perish wretchedness of all, / If in defiance of the law we cross / A monarch's will?" To the contrary, Antigone feels that Creon's decree should be disobeyed because it violates the basic rules of loving family relationships and the eternal laws of the Greek Gods. Ismene, trying to use reason, continues to object to Antigone's plan and cautions Antigone that she will likely be killed if she follows through on it. Sophocles shows that Antigone is making her choice to break the rules partly on tradition, but mostly on emotion. Antigone scornfully replies to Ismene, "Go thine own way; myself will bury him, / How sweet to die in such employ, to rest— / Sister and brother linked in love's embrace— / A sinless sinner, banned awhile on earth, / But by the dead commended; and with them I shall abide for ever. As for thee, / Scorn if thou wilt, the eternal laws of Heaven" (Sophocles). For Antigone, the unfair rule of a vengeful but victorious leader may be rightfully broken so that the more important

rules of family and faith can prevail. Should the heart rule the head? Sophocles shows that Antigone, whatever her choice, will have to live, or die, with the consequences of her actions.

In his novel *Animal Farm,* George Orwell also deals with the importance of rules to social order. As was the case for Antigone in Thebes, the rules of Animal Farm seem to be justifiably broken, but for different reasons and with different consequences. Orwell uses this story of farm animals to explore the limits of rules and the uses of power. After the animals' initial overthrow of Mr. Jones's rule, Snowball and Napoleon vie for leadership. A debate over the building of the windmill precedes what is supposed to be a democratic vote by all the animals. To the animals' surprise, the democratic rules of debate and voting are violated when the meeting turns into a military-style coup as Napoleon uses his trained dogs to viciously attack Snowball and chase him off the farm. Having seized power, Napoleon immediately changes the existing rules so he can maintain iron-fisted control. "He [Napoleon] announced that from now on the Sunday-morning meetings would come to an end.... In future all questions relating to the working of the farm would be settled by a special committee of pigs, presided over by himself" (Orwell). Later, Napoleon sends Squeaker around the farm to explain the new rules. Squeaker tells the animals, "No one believes more firmly than Comrade Napoleon that all animals are equal. He would be only too happy to let you make your decisions for yourselves. But sometimes you might make the wrong decisions, comrades, and then where should we be?" (Orwell). Previously, the animals had justifiably broken rules when they overthrew their human masters. The animals are eventually subjected to the same type of autocratic control that they had sought to overthrow.

In summary, the main characters of both texts think they are right to overthrow what they see as unfair rules. That said, the breaking of rules may result in dire consequences. For Antigone, death may be the punishment she pays for disobeying Creon's edict. For the creatures living on Animal Farm, the breaking of the rules merely changes the leadership of the farm, but it does not improve the lives of the animals. Both Sophocles and Orwell seem to asking readers if there is any chance of a middle ground, a true compromise, and seem to suggest that this tension will never be resolved. In short, rules may be justifiably broken, but not without unintended and often unpleasant consequences.

NOTES

**Works Cited**

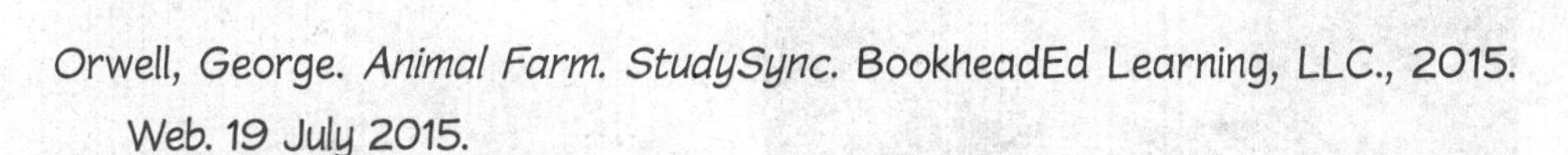

Orwell, George. *Animal Farm. StudySync.* BookheadEd Learning, LLC., 2015. Web. 19 July 2015.

Sophocles. *Antigone. StudySync.* BookheadEd Learning, LLC., 2015. Web. 19 July 2015.

## THINK QUESTIONS

1. What is the central or main idea of this essay? How do you know? Cite textual evidence to support your ideas.
2. How is the text in "Breaking the Rules" organized?
3. What types of evidence does the writer provide in the body paragraphs of this literary analysis?
4. As you consider the writing prompt, which selections, Blasts, or other resources would you like to use to create your own literary analysis?
5. Based on what you have read, listened to, or researched, how would you answer the question: *When is it appropriate to challenge the rules?* What are some examples of situations in which you think rules should be broken?

NOTES

# PREWRITE

CA-CCSS: CA.RL.9-10.1, CA.RL.9-10.2, CA.RL.9-10.3, CA.W.9-10.1a, CA.W.9-10.1b, CA.W.9-10.4, CA.W.9-10.6, CA.W.9-10.9a, CA.W.9-10.10, CA.SL.9-10.1a, CA.SL.9-10.1b, CA.SL.9-10.1c, CA.L.9-10.4b

## WRITING PROMPT

Rules have played an important role in societies around the world and across the ages. What the rules are, why they matter, how they are broken, and why some people feel they must break them are central concerns in many texts from this unit, which seeks to answer the essential question, *When is it appropriate to challenge the rules?* Write a literary analysis of two selections you have read during the unit, examining how the authors explore the issue of when it is appropriate to challenge the rules.

Your literary analysis should include:

- an introduction that
  - › presents a reasonable claim, expressed in a clear thesis statement
  - › names the author and title of each text you have selected to support your claim
- body paragraphs that
  - › present a thorough analysis of your claim
  - › contain textual evidence and details to support your claim
  - › demonstrate a logical organization of ideas
- a conclusion paragraph that
  - › restates your thesis statement
  - › effectively wraps up your essay
  - › leaves your reader with a lasting impression, perhaps through an interesting final thought

You have been reading stories and other texts that feature people breaking the rules. You have also been learning about literary analysis as a form of argumentative writing. Now you will use argumentative writing techniques to compose your own literary analysis in response to the prompt.

NOTES

Remember that literary analysis asks you to make a claim or take a position on a topic and then to identify, evaluate, and provide textual evidence that offers reasonable support for the claim. Consider the situation in George Orwell's *Animal Farm*. What rules existed? How did the characters challenge the rules? Why did they believe that it was necessary to break the rules? What were the results of breaking the rules? Think about not only the message that Orwell conveys but how he conveys it.

Make a "mind map" of answers to such questions for three texts you have encountered in this unit. **You must use at least one work of fiction or drama, although the second text may be fiction, drama, poetry, or nonfiction.** Note that in some texts, while the rules might not actually have been broken, the author might strongly suggest that they should have been. As you write down your ideas, consider whether the author presents a fair case for breaking the rules. Do you agree with the situations presented in the text? Why or why not? Determining the answers to these questions will help you craft the claim of your argumentative essay. Also look for patterns that emerge. Do these texts have anything in common? What important differences do they have? Look for these patterns to help you build support for your main claim. Use this model to help you get started with your own mind map:

Model Text: *Animal Farm* by George Orwell

**The Rules:** Animals should obey their human masters.

**How the Rules Were/Should Have Been Challenged:** The animals have overthrown their human leader, Mr. Jones, to establish democratic rule on the farm. Snowball and Napoleon then vie for leadership.

**Reasons It Was Appropriate to Challenge the Rules:** Democratic rule was enacted to ensure that the farm ran properly and fairly, under animal (rather than human) control.

**Results of Challenging/Not Challenging the Rules:** When the power-hungry Napoleon believes that Snowball is making the wrong decision about the windmill, he instructs his trained dogs to chase Snowball from the farm. He then seizes an autocratic role and changes the rules of the farm, so that he will make all final decisions.

**Author's Message:** Not everyone will have the same point of view about what rules in a new society should be established and enforced. Challenging unjust rules does not always lead to the establishment of more just ones.

**How Author Conveys the Message:** Orwell shows, through the animals' actions, how human beings struggle for power over who controls the rules. He demonstrates that it is an ugly business by depicting how some individuals get impatient with democracy.

NOTES

# SKILL: THESIS STATEMENT

## DEFINE

The thesis statement is the most important sentence in an argumentative essay, such as a literary analysis, because it introduces what the writer is going to explore or attempt to prove in the essay or analysis. The thesis statement expresses the writer's central or main idea about that topic, which is the position the writer will develop in the body of the essay. The thesis statement usually appears in the essay's introductory paragraph and is often the introduction's last sentence. The rest of the paragraphs in the essay all support the thesis statement with specific details, facts, evidence, quotations, and examples. The thesis statement should reappear in some form in the essay's concluding paragraph.

## IDENTIFICATION AND APPLICATION

A thesis statement:

- makes a clear statement about the writer's central idea.
- lets the reader know what to expect in the body of the essay.
- responds fully and completely to an essay prompt.
- is presented in the introduction and restated in the conclusion.
- is a work-in-progress and should be revised and improved, as needed, during the early stages of the writing process.

## MODEL

The following is the introductory paragraph from the student model essay "Breaking the Rules":

> *Rules are often thought of as the bricks and mortar that people use to construct the societies they live in. Rules we are told keep the wheels of*

NOTES

society turning, provide people with basic necessities, keep peace and order, and secure the well-being of citizens. Without rules, nations and whole cultures will likely descend into chaos and eventual self-destruction. Yet rules can be perverted and used to violate the needs and rights of the people they are meant to serve. **Sophocles's play *Antigone* and George Orwell's novel *Animal Farm* provide examples of events and situations in which it is clear that sometimes rules may rightly be challenged and broken, although not without consequences.**

Notice the bold-faced thesis statement. This student's thesis statement responds to the prompt, identifying the selections he will analyze, the authors of those selections, and the point he will be making about the selections. It reminds readers of the topic of the essay—in this case, how two authors examine the issue of when it is appropriate to break the rules. It also specifically states the writer's particular central or main idea about that topic. In this writer's view, these authors show that in certain situations rules should be broken but consequences should be expected.

## PRACTICE

Draft a thesis statement with pen and paper that states your main idea in a clear and engaging way. Be sure that your thesis statement addresses the prompt. When you are done writing, switch papers with a partner to evaluate each other's work. How clearly did the writer state his or her claim in the thesis statement? Does the thesis statement address the topic posed in the prompt? Does the thesis statement clearly set a focus for the rest of the essay? Offer suggestions, and remember that they are most helpful when they are informative and constructive.

# SKILL: ORGANIZE ARGUMENTATIVE WRITING

## DEFINE

The purpose of argumentative writing focused on literary analysis is to make a claim or take a position on a topic, and then to identify, evaluate, and present relevant textual evidence that supports the position. To do this effectively, writers need to organize and present their claims, topics, ideas, facts, details, and other information in a logical way that makes it easy for readers to follow and understand.

Students are often asked to write argumentative essays that analyze literary texts as part of their studies in English language arts classes. A common method for writing a strong argumentative essay is organizing the writing using the **five-paragraph strategy.** As you saw in the introductory lesson, this consists of an **introductory paragraph** that presents the topic and the writer's position in a **thesis statement.** The introduction is then followed by **three body paragraphs,** each of which presents evidentiary details and ideas that support some aspect of the essay's thesis. The fifth paragraph is a **conclusion** that provides a unique restatement of the thesis, reviews the evidence presented, and ends with a concluding sentence that wraps up the analysis. The five-paragraph approach is straightforward, concise, and effective. However, it is not the only organizational structure that may be used to write a strong argumentative essay.

The content of the essay—that is, the type of prompt the writer is responding to, the nature of the textual evidence to be presented for support and analysis, and the characteristics of the selections to be analyzed—must also be considered in choosing an overall **organizational structure** that suits the topic and the literary texts a writer plans to analyze. For example, in comparing the treatment of a topic from two historical novels, the writer might decide that a **sequential** or chronological structure might work best since events can then be discussed in the order they occurred. On the other hand, if the writer is analyzing the similarity and differences of the actions of characters in resolving conflicts from several short stories or plays, a **compare and contrast** structure might be the most effective organizational method for an

argumentative essay. Other organizational structures include **problem and solution** and **cause-and-effect.** It is important to remember that while an essay or a paragraph may use an overall organizational method, it may be necessary to introduce another organizational technique to get across an important point in a particular section of the analysis.

## IDENTIFICATION AND APPLICATION

- When selecting an organizational structure, writers must consider the purpose of their writing. They often ask themselves questions about the nature of the writing task in which they are engaging. They might ask themselves the following questions:
  - Can I express my thoughts effectively within a five-paragraph structure?
  - What claim am I making about the topic?
  - Am I comparing and contrasting different viewpoints held by different characters about the same topic, issue, or conflict?
  - Would it make sense to relay events in the order they occurred?
  - What is the problem and what solutions did the characters find or the events lead to?
  - Do any natural cause-and-effect relationships emerge from the evidence that supports my claim?

- Writers often choose specific words to create connections between details and signal the organizational structure being used:
  - Sequential order: *first, next, then, finally, last, initially, ultimately*
  - Cause and effect: *because, accordingly, as a result, effect, so*
  - Compare and contrast: *like, unlike, also, both, similarly, although, while, but, however*

- Sometimes, within the overall structure, writers may find it necessary to organize individual paragraphs using other structures—for instance, a paragraph that compares and contrasts might benefit from a quick summary of events presented in chronological order. Be careful that such mixed strategies do not muddy the overall organization.

## MODEL

After completing his prewriting mind map and selecting two texts from the unit to explore in his literary analysis, the writer of the Student Model "Breaking the Rules" understood that he would have to compare and contrast characters or individuals both within and across texts.

For example, the writer used a three-column chart to compare and contrast ideas that emerged from both *Antigone* and *Animal Farm* about the issue of when it is appropriate to break the rules.

| POINT OF COMPARISON/ CONTRAST | *ANTIGONE* | *ANIMAL FARM* |
|---|---|---|
| **Reasons for challenging the rules** | beliefs about the fate of unburied, family obligations, laws of the Greek gods | the creation of a democratic society |
| **Consequences for challenging the rules** | possible death | an alternative government that is just as corrupt and dictatorial as the one that was overthrown |
| **Author's overall message** | rules may rightly be challenged but harsh consequences may result | rules may rightly be challenged but harsh consequences may result |

The information assembled in the chart helped the author develop the claim of his literary analysis, which is restated and elaborated on in the conclusion:

> *In summary, the main characters of* **both** *texts think they are right to overthrow what they see as unfair rules. That said, the breaking of rules may result in dire consequences. For Antigone, death may be the punishment she pays for disobeying Creon's edict. For the creatures living on Animal Farm, the breaking of the rules merely changes the leadership of the farm, but it does not improve the lives of the animals.* **Both** *Sophocles and Orwell seem to be asking readers if there is any chance of a middle ground, a true compromise, and seem to suggest that this tension will never be resolved. In short, rules may be justifiably broken, but not without unintended and often unpleasant consequences.*

Note that the word "both" is used twice to signal important comparisons between how challenging the rules is treated in the texts and between the authors' overall messages about when it is appropriate to challenge the rules.

In addition, as part of his analysis for *Antigone*, the writer found that he would need to compare and contrast the viewpoints of Ismene and Antigone about whether or not Creon's decree concerning the burial of Polyneices should be obeyed or broken. He created a Pro (disobey the decree) and Con (obey the decree) diagram to compare and contrast these two characters' points of view:

***Ismene***
***Obey Creon's Decree***

- Women must always follow rules of male leaders.
- Will be stoned to dealth if the decree is disobeyed.

***Antigone***
***Disobey Creon's Decree***

- The spirits of the unburied can't find peace.
- Family relationships obligate sisters to bury brothers.
- Buriel is commanded by the laws of the Greek gods.

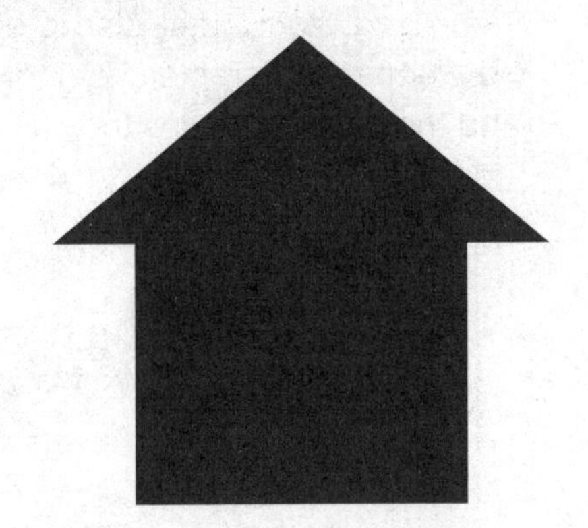

As the information in this graphic makes clear, the writer identified different arguments on each side of the question of whether or not it is appropriate to challenge the rules and then used these arguments to structure the third body paragraph of his analysis. For example, he writes:

> Ismene believes that it is the role of Greek citizens, especially women, to follow the rules set down by the male leaders of their society. Ismene warns, "Shall we not perish wretchedness of all, / If in defiance of the law we cross / A monarch's will?" **To the contrary,** Antigone feels that Creon's decree should be disobeyed because it violates the basic rules of loving family relationships and the eternal laws of the Greek Gods.

In this passage, the phrase "To the contrary" signals that the writer will explore a contrast between one of Ismene's beliefs (which he noted in the first bullet in the "Con" section of the graphic) and two of Antigone's beliefs (which he noted in the second and third bullets in the "Pro" section of the graphic).

## PRACTICE

Compare and contrast the two texts you have selected for use in your argumentative essay. Using a three-column chart like the one above, fill in the information you gathered about each text during the Prewrite stage of the writing process as well as any additional information about the texts you would like to include. When you are done writing, switch charts with a partner to evaluate each other's work. Are the ideas appropriate for each section of the chart? Offer suggestions, and remember that they are most helpful when they are informative and constructive.

Note that you can also use a Microsoft Word *SmartArt* graphic like the one you have just studied, a traditional Venn diagram, or a graphic organizer of your own design to organize individual paragraphs within your essay. For example, a Venn Diagram might be effective if you choose to analyze points of comparison and contrast between two characters or individuals in the same text. You might also create a flowchart that shows the relationship between the characters' or individuals' decisions to break the rules (causes) and the consequences they faced as a result (effects).

# SKILL: SUPPORTING DETAILS

## DEFINE

In argumentative writing, writers develop their main idea with relevant evidence called supporting details. These details can include any fact, definition, concrete information, example, or quotation that helps to prove the author's claim and is closely related to the thesis statement, or main idea. Relevant supporting details are the key to the success of a writer's argument. They make the argument more convincing and persuasive to the reader, help develop the ideas the author presents, and clarify the writer's understanding and interpretation of the text. Without reasons and relevant evidence, the writer would simply be stating his or her opinion about a theme or a central idea.

## IDENTIFICATION AND APPLICATION

For a literary analysis:

- Provide details in the form of evidence found in the literary text or texts being discussed. Direct quotations, followed by the writer's analysis of the quotations in connection to the thesis, make the strongest evidence.
- Use only details that will help prove your point. Too many details, or unorganized details, can confuse a point rather than prove it.
- Use the details to develop the main claim of the paper—often called the thesis—over the course of the entire text. Every detail chosen should support the thesis.

## MODEL

The most common use of argumentative writing, such as a literary analysis, is to convince readers that the writer's stand on an issue or view of a topic—his or her thesis—is the correct one and should be adopted by the reader. The best way to convince readers of the correctness of a thesis is to provide plenty of details that support it.

A common mistake in student writing is to venture off topic and introduce details that may be interesting, but are not **relevant,** or clearly related to the argument being developed. It is important to always consider how a detail is related to the thesis. If a connection cannot be drawn, the detail may need to be deleted. Including too many irrelevant details will lead many readers to find a writer's thesis unconvincing.

In *The Whisperers: Private Life in Stalin's Russia,* by Orlando Figes, all of the details unite to prove the author's thesis: that Communist citizens were brainwashed to support and take part in atrocities against their countrymen as their "revolutionary duty." Figes makes a point of telling individual stories to engage readers' emotions. He begins the text with a personal story that shows the cruelty of the "collectivizers":

> **Klavdiia Rublyova** was born in 1913, the third of **eleven children** in a peasant family in the Irbei region of Krasnoiarsk in Siberia. **Her mother died in 1924, while giving birth, leaving her father, Ilia, to bring up all the children on his own.** An enterprising man, Ilia took advantage of the NEP [New Economic Policy] to branch out from farming to market gardening. **He grew poppy seeds and cucumbers, which could easily be tended by his young children. For this he was branded a 'kulak', arrested and imprisoned, and later sent to a labour camp,** leaving his children in the care of Klavdiia, who was then aged just seventeen. The children were deprived of all their father's property: the house, which he had built, was taken over by the village Soviet, while the horses, cows and sheep and the farm tools were transferred to the kolkhoz.

The text as a whole focuses on the impact of Stalin's Five Year Plan on many "kulaks" and on the motivations of the many "collectivizers" who persecuted them. Why, then, does the author include so many details about just one individual, Klavdiia Rublyova, and her family? When eliciting reader emotions, one personal story can be more powerful than a list of facts about the large nameless numbers who suffered. Figes focuses on a single family in which a father creatively tried to feed his eleven children, and as a result, was "branded a 'kulak', arrested and imprisoned, and later sent to a labour camp." This one powerful example illustrates for readers in a vivid, compelling way the unfairness and cruelty many peasants experienced at the hands of the collectivizers.

Note that it is important for writers of formal academic essays, such as a literary analysis, to work to maintain **objectivity.** That is, in a formal paper, writers should back up the details they include with strong analysis and think carefully before including words with specific connotations, such as "branded." "Branded" carries a negative connotation and suggests that the author condemns what happened to the "kulaks" and feels that it was extremely unfair.

Writers might begin to list the details they will use in a graphic organizer before writing about them. This sort of forethought helps writers to avoid the mistake of including details that do not support the thesis. Look at this graphic organizer, which shows how the details included in the passage from Figes's text support his thesis:

| DETAIL | WHAT POINT DOES THIS DETAIL MAKE? | HOW DOES THIS DETAIL SUPPORT THE THESIS? |
|---|---|---|
| Her mother died in 1924, while giving birth, leaving her father, Ilia, to bring up all the children on his own. | Ilia Rublyova faced challenging circumstances, and likely struggled to provide for his family. | This detail shows the challenges Rublyova faced and why he likely branched out from farming to market gardening, for which he was punished so severely. |
| He grew poppy seeds and cucumbers, which could easily be tended by his young children. | The crops he grew were modest, as they could be cared for by his children, and likely yielded only a small amount additional income. | This detail shows why the severe consequences that Ilia Rublyova faced as a result of his pursuit of market gardening were unjust and completely out of proportion to his "crime." |
| The children were deprived of all their father's property: the house, which he had built, was taken over by the village Soviet, while the horses, cows and sheep and the farm tools were transferred to the kolkhoz. | The Siberian peasants were treated cruelly and unfairly during this period in history. | This detail shows how inhumane citizens under Stalin became. |

## PRACTICE

Complete a graphic organizer such as the one above with details from each selection you have chosen to discuss in your literary analysis. Use the information you gathered in the Prewrite stage and the Organize Argumentative Writing lesson. Be sure that your details make relevant points that directly support your thesis statement. When you are done writing, switch completed charts with a partner to evaluate each other's work. How clear are the details on the chart? Are the details relevant? How well did the writer explain what point each detail makes? Do the details provide strong support for the writer's thesis statement? Offer suggestions for improvement, and remember that they are most helpful when they are informative and constructive.

NOTES

# PLAN

CA-CCSS: CA.RL.9-10.1, CA.W.9-10.1a, CA.W.9-10.1b, CA.W.9-10.4, CA.W.9-10.5, CA.W.9-10.6, CA.W.9-10.9a, CA.W.9-10.10, CA.SL.9-10.1a, CA.SL.9-10.1d, CA.SL.9-10.2, CA.SL.9-10.3

## WRITING PROMPT

Rules have played an important role in societies around the world and across the ages. What the rules are, why they matter, how they are broken, and why some people feel they must break them are central concerns in many texts from this unit, which seeks to answer the essential question, *When is it appropriate to challenge the rules?* Write a literary analysis of two selections you have read during the unit, examining how the authors explore the issue of when it is appropriate to challenge the rules.

Your literary analysis should include:

- an introduction that
  - › presents a reasonable claim, expressed in a clear thesis statement
  - › names the author and title of each text you have selected to support your claim
- body paragraphs that
  - › present a thorough analysis of your claim
  - › contain textual evidence and details to support your claim
  - › demonstrate a logical organization of ideas
- a conclusion paragraph that
  - › restates your thesis statement
  - › effectively wraps up your essay
  - › leaves your reader with a lasting impression, perhaps through an interesting final thought

As you begin to plan your literary analysis, use your prewriting and what you learned about addressing the needs of your audience and establishing your purpose, creating an effective thesis statement or claim, clearly and logically organizing the information and ideas you include, and strongly supporting your claim. First, assemble your thesis statement, your brainstorming mind

map from the Prewrite stage, your completed three-column chart from the Organize Argumentative Writing lesson, and your completed graphic organizer from the Supporting Details lesson. Then, create a road map to use for writing your literary analysis.

Consider the following questions as you develop your paragraph topics and supporting details in the road map:

- How do the characters or individuals in the two texts you will analyze gain an understanding of the rules?
- To what extent do the characters or individuals in these texts think that the rules matter?
- What beliefs or ideals do the characters or individuals in these texts hold to be most important?
- What kind of relationships do the characters or individuals in these texts have with those in power?
- What situations do the characters or individuals face that cause them to consider challenging the rules?
- How do the characters or individuals break the rules? If they don't break the rules, why not?
- Do you think it is necessary for these characters or individuals to break the rules? Why or why not?
- What consequences do these characters or individuals face as a result of breaking or of not breaking the rules?

Use this model to get started with your road map:

**Literary Analysis Road Map**

Thesis statement: Sophocles's play *Antigone* and George Orwell's novel *Animal Farm* provide examples of events and situations in which it is clear that sometimes rules may rightly be challenged and broken, although not without consequences.

Paragraph 1 Topic: Rules are intended to keep society in order and help meet the needs of citizens.

Supporting Detail #1: Rules are necessary to prevent chaos and destruction of society.

Supporting Detail #2: Rules sometimes violate the needs and rights of those they are meant to serve, as seen in Sophocles's play *Antigone* and George Orwell's novel *Animal Farm*.

Paragraph 2 Topic: In *Antigone,* Antigone must decide if she will obey King Creon's decree or break the rules by burying her brother, Polyneices.

Supporting Detail #1: Her brother Eteocles has been buried with the full rituals of a Greek citizen and soldier because he fought for Thebes, but Creon has ordered that Polyneices, who fought against Thebes, should remain unburied

Supporting Detail #2: Leaving Polyneices' body unburied will condemn his spirit to roam the land without peace.

Paragraph 3 Topic: Sisters Antigone and Ismene are at odds about what is the right action to take.

Supporting Detail #1: Ismene believes that it is the role of Greek citizens, especially women, to follow the rules set down by the male leaders of their society. She is driven by reason, stating: "Shall we not perish wretchedness of all, / If in defiance of the law we cross / A monarch's will?"

Supporting Detail #2: Antigone feels that Creon's decree violates the basic rules of loving family relationships and the eternal laws of the Greek gods. She is driven by emotion, telling her sister, "Go thine own way; myself will bury him, / How sweet to die in such employ, to rest— / Sister and brother linked in love's embrace— / A sinless sinner, banned awhile on earth, / But by the dead commended; and with them I shall abide for ever. As for thee, / Scorn if thou wilt, the eternal laws of Heaven." Sophocles shows that Antigone's choice will have consequences, no matter which course of action she chooses.

Paragraph 4 Topic: In *Animal Farm,* Orwell uses the story of farm animals to explore the limits of rules and the uses of power.

Supporting Detail #1: After the animals overthrow the human Mr. Jones's dictatorial rule, they attempt to establish a democracy, although Snowball and Napoleon vie for leadership.

Supporting Detail #2: During a debate over the building of the windmill, Napoleon enacts a military-style coup and seizes power of the farm, so that he will make all final decisions on behalf of the other animals. "He [Napoleon] announced that from now on the Sunday-morning meetings would come to an end . . . . In future all questions relating to the working of thefarm would be settled by a special committee of pigs, presided over by himself."

Paragraph 5 Topic: The main characters of both texts think they are right to overthrow what they see as unfair rules, but they will have to suffer the consequences of this choice.

Supporting Detail #1: Antigone faces death as punishment for disobeying Creon's edict.

Supporting Detail #2: In *Animal Farm,* the overthrow of human leadership causes great change, but it does not seem to improve the lives of the animals.

# SKILL: INTRODUCTIONS

## DEFINE

The **introduction** is the opening paragraph or section of a literary analysis or other nonfiction text. The introduction of a literary analysis identifies the texts and the topic to be discussed. It almost always states the writer's **thesis,** the central **claim** that will be developed in the remainder of the essay. However, in some cases the thesis may be implicit in the introduction, rather than directly stated, and then stated explicitly later in the essay. The introduction previews the relevant evidence that will support the thesis and appear in the body of the text. The introduction is also the place where most writers include a "hook" that is intended to connect with and engage readers.

## IDENTIFICATION AND APPLICATION

- In a literary analysis, the introduction is the section in which the writer identifies the texts and topic to be discussed. Once readers have that information, they can concentrate on the writer's claim, which is expressed in the **thesis statement.**
- A literary analysis is a form of argument, so the writer's claim is an important part of the introduction. The claim is a direct statement of the writer's opinion about, or interpretation of, the texts under discussion. By stating the thesis or claim in the introduction, the writer lets readers know the ideas he or she will explore in the body of the analysis. Establishing a claim here also allows readers to form their own opinions, which they can then measure against the writer's thesis or claim as they read the literary analysis.
- Sometimes a thesis statement or claim will be implicit in the introduction and stated explicitly later. This may happen when a writer wishes to establish a foundation of evidence for the thesis before introducing it. Usually, however, the thesis is expressed as part of the introduction, often as the last sentence of the introductory paragraph or section.

- Another use of the introduction is to provide a preview of the supporting evidence that will follow in the body of the text. By using the introduction to hint at key details, the writer can establish an effective argument, increasing the likelihood that readers will agree with his or her claim.
- A "hook" in the opening of an essay is something that grabs a reader and draws him or her in. In other words, a good hook engages the interest of readers and makes them want to keep reading. The hook should appeal to the audience and help readers connect to the topic in a meaningful way so that they will take the writer's claim seriously. An effective hook might include:
  - a quotation
  - a question
  - a brief anecdote
  - a strong statement
  - a connection to the reader or to life
  - a startling statistic

## MODEL

When setting up an argument, introductions can take many forms and have different tones. Some texts open with direct questions that the writer wants to answer. Others might begin in an adversarial way, challenging the audience from the beginning to consider the writer's point of view. The introduction of Patrick Henry's *Speech to the Second Virginia Convention,* to highlight another example, shows the most charming way possible for a speaker to tell an audience that he wholeheartedly disagrees with them:

> **Mr. President, no man thinks more highly than I do of the patriotism, as well as abilities, of the very worthy gentlemen who have just addressed the House.** But different men often see the same subject in different lights; and, therefore, I hope it will not be thought disrespectful to those gentlemen if, entertaining as I do, **opinions of a character very opposite to theirs, I shall speak forth my sentiments freely, and without reserve.** This is no time for ceremony. The question before the House is one of awful moment to this country. For my own part, I consider it as nothing less than a question of freedom or slavery; and **in proportion to the magnitude of the subject ought to be the freedom of the debate. It is only in this way that we can hope to arrive at truth,** and fulfill the great responsibility which we hold to God and our country. **Should I keep back my opinions at such a time, through fear of giving offence, I should consider myself as guilty of treason towards my**

NOTES

***country,** and of an act of disloyalty toward the majesty of heaven, which I revere above all earthly kings.*

Henry starts by establishing his respect for the speakers who "just addressed the House," a move that encourages the audience to show him the same respect. This respect is very important because the speaker's thesis, which he does not explicitly state until later in his speech, will consist of "opinions of a character very opposite to theirs." The fact that Henry declares his disagreement in an inoffensive but direct manner conveys a sense of confidence and authority that serves to "hook," or capture the interest and attention of his audience.

Henry also knows his audience admires patriotism and allegiance to the nation's cause, so he emphasizes that his views, though widely opposed to many others, should be considered because they are in fact the *most* patriotic. He lets listeners know that he will speak "freely and without reserve," for a true patriot knows that "in proportion to the magnitude of the subject ought to be the freedom of the debate. It is only in this way that we can hope to arrive at truth." Henry positions himself as a respectful, patriotic citizen even as he lets his colleagues know he disagrees with many of them. To be less than honest would cause him to feel "guilty of treason" toward his country. While many of the people in this audience may have disregarded Henry right from the start because of his message, Henry uses the introduction of his speech to create a forum in which disagreement can be expressed both respectfully and freely and to garner interest in his controversial message supporting revolution.

## PRACTICE

Write an introduction for your essay that includes the thesis statement you have been developing as well as a hook to capture your readers' interest. Trade with a peer review partner when you are finished and offer feedback on each other's introductions. Remember that suggestions for improvement are most helpful when they are supportive and kind.

# SKILL: BODY PARAGRAPHS AND TRANSITIONS

## DEFINE

**Body paragraphs** are the section of the essay between the introduction and conclusion paragraphs. This is where you support your thesis statement by developing your main points with evidence from the text and analysis. Typically, each body paragraph will focus on one main point or idea to avoid confusing the reader. The main idea or focus of each body paragraph must help develop and support the thesis statement.

It's important to structure your body paragraph clearly. One strategy for structuring the body paragraph for an argumentative essay is the following:

**Write a topic sentence:** The topic sentence is the first sentence of your body paragraph and clearly states the main idea or focus of the paragraph. In the first body paragraph, the topic sentence should connect your thesis statement to the first set of evidence you will use to support the thesis statement.

**Provide evidence:** Be sure to support your topic sentence with evidence. Evidence can be a summary of relevant facts, concrete details, quotations, definitions, or other information and examples.

**Analyze/Explain:** After presenting evidence to support your topic sentence, you will need to analyze that evidence and explain how it supports your topic sentence and, in effect, your thesis.

**Repeat, as needed:** Use the process above for each body paragraph you add, since you may find that you want to provide another piece of related evidence and analysis. Be sure that all the evidence in each body paragraph supports the same idea.

**Concluding sentence:** After presenting your evidence in a body paragraph, you need to wrap up your main idea. In addition, this sentence should help lead to the next body paragraph or to the conclusion.

**Transitions** are connecting words and phrases that clarify the relationships among ideas in a text. Transitions work at three different levels: 1) within a sentence, 2) within a paragraph, and 3) between paragraphs, providing an organizational structure.

## IDENTIFICATION AND APPLICATION

- Body paragraphs of an argumentative essay appear between the introduction and conclusion paragraphs. Body paragraphs provide the evidence and explanation needed to support the thesis statement. Typically, writers develop one main idea per body paragraph.
  - › Topic sentences clearly state the main idea of that paragraph.
  - › Evidence consists of relevant facts, concrete details, quotations, definitions, or other information and examples.
  - › Analysis and explanation are needed to explain how the evidence supports the topic sentence.
  - › The conclusion sentence wraps up the main point and transitions to the next body paragraph.

- Transitional words are a necessary element of a successful piece of argumentative writing.
  - › Transitional words help readers understand the text structure of an argumentative text. Here are some transitional words that are frequently used in three different text structures:
    - › Cause-effect: *because, accordingly, as a result, effect, so, for, since*
    - › Compare-contrast: *like, unlike, also, both, similarly, although, while, but, however, whereas, conversely, meanwhile, on the contrary, and yet, still*
    - › Chronological order: *first, next, then, finally, last, initially, ultimately*

- Transitional words and phrases help authors make connections between words within a sentence. Conjunctions such as *and*, *or*, and *but* and prepositions such as *with*, *beyond*, *inside*, show the relationships between words. Transitions help readers understand how words fit together to make meaning.
- Transitional words help readers understand the flow of ideas and concepts in a paragraph. Some of the most useful transitions are words that indicate that the ideas in one paragraph are building on or adding to those in another. Examples include: *furthermore, therefore, in addition, moreover, by extension, in order to,* and so on.
- Authors of argumentative texts focused on literary analysis use transitions to help readers connect one author to another and one text to another and to recognize the relationships among ideas. Transitions are a key

organizational tool for essays like this. Transitions to connect paragraphs can appear in the concluding sentence of one paragraph and/or in the beginning sentence of the next.

## MODEL

The Student Model essay, "Breaking the Rules," uses a three-body-paragraph structure to develop the essay's thesis statement. The writer provides transitions to help the reader connect ideas within sentences and paragraphs, as well as between paragraphs.

Reread the body paragraphs from the Student Model "Breaking the Rules." Look closely at the structure and note the transitional words in bold. Consider the essay's thesis: "Sophocles's play *Antigone* and George Orwell's novel *Animal Farm* provide examples of events and situations in which it is clear that sometimes rules may rightly be challenged and broken, although not without consequences." How does the main point expressed in each paragraph's topic sentence reinforce this thesis? How do the details contained in each paragraph effectively develop its main point? How do transitional words help you to understand the connections between ideas?

> **In the opening scene of *Antigone*,** Sophocles introduces the audience to the initial conflict of the play: whether or not to obey King Creon's decree. Antigone and Ismene's brothers—Polyneices and Eteocles—have killed each other during battle. Eteocles, who fought on the side of the victorious city of Thebes, has been buried with the full rituals of a Greek citizen and soldier. **However,** Creon, the new king of Thebes, has ordered that Polyneices, who fought against Thebes, should remain unburied. His body is to remain on the open battlefield, and his spirit is condemned to roam the land without peace. Antigone has asked to meet her sister outside the gates of Thebes to plea for help in taking Polyneices' body for proper burial. Should Antigone break the law or not? **This is the problem Sophocles explores.**
>
> **Immediately,** the two sisters begin to argue over the whether or not Creon's decree should be followed. As the sisters show their differences, the audience gets a chance to see both sides of the argument. Ismene believes that it is the role of Greek citizens, especially women, to follow the rules set down by the male leaders of their society. Ismene warns, "Shall we not perish wretchedness of all, / If in defiance of the law we cross / A monarch's will?" **To the contrary,** Antigone feels that Creon's decree should be disobeyed

NOTES

because it violates the basic rules of loving family relationships and the eternal laws of the Greek Gods. Ismene, trying to use reason, continues to object to Antigone's plan and cautions Antigone that she will likely be killed if she follows through on it. **Sophocles shows that Antigone is making her choice to break the rules partly on tradition, but mostly on emotion.** Antigone scornfully replies to Ismene, "Go thine own way; myself will bury him, / How sweet to die in such employ, to rest— / Sister and brother linked in love's embrace— / A sinless sinner, banned awhile on earth, / But by the dead commended; and with them I shall abide for ever. As for thee, / Scorn if thou wilt, the eternal laws of Heaven" (Sophocles). For Antigone, the unfair rule of a vengeful but victorious leader may be rightfully broken so that the more important rules of family and faith can prevail. Should the heart rule the head? **Sophocles shows that Antigone, whatever her choice, will have to live, or die, with the consequences of her actions.**

**In his novel *Animal Farm,*** George Orwell **also** deals with the importance of rules to social order. **As it was for Antigone in Thebes, the rules of Animal Farm seem to be justifiably broken, but** for different reasons and with different consequences. Orwell uses this story of farm animals to explore the limits of rules and the uses of power. **After** the animals' initial overthrow of Mr. Jones's rule, Snowball and Napoleon vie for leadership. A debate over the building of the windmill precedes what is supposed to be a democratic vote by all the animals. **To the animals' surprise,** the democratic rules of debate and voting are violated when the meeting turns into a military-style coup as Napoleon uses his trained dogs to viciously attack Snowball and chase him off the farm. Having seized power, Napoleon immediately changes the existing rules so he can maintain iron-fisted control. "He [Napoleon] announced that from now on the Sunday-morning meetings would come to an end.... In future all questions relating to the working of the farm would be settled by a special committee of pigs, presided over by himself" (Orwell). **Later,** Napoleon sends Squeaker around the farm to explain the new rules. Squeaker tells the animals, "No one believes more firmly than Comrade Napoleon that all animals are equal. He would be only too happy to let you make your decisions for yourselves. But sometimes you might make the wrong decisions, comrades, and then where should we be?" (Orwell). **Previously,** the animals had justifiably broken rules when they overthrew their human masters. The animals are eventually subjected to the same type of autocratic control that they had sought to overthrow.

The first two body paragraphs of the Student Model are concerned with developing ideas from *Antigone* that support the thesis statement expressed in the introduction. The first body paragraph begins by stating, "In the opening scene of *Antigone*, we are introduced to the initial conflict of the play: whether or not to obey King Creon's decree." This **topic sentence** clearly establishes the main idea of this body paragraph, which is that a conflict exists. This topic sentence is immediately followed by **evidence** in the form of specific details from the play that introduces all the main characters and the key events that lead up to the focus of the first scene. The writer closes the paragraph by pointing out the author's purpose, which to explore this question: "Should Antigone break the law or not?"

The second body paragraph narrows the focus to the specific terms of the conflict by recounting Ismene's and Antigone's positions concerning Creon's decree. The student writer summarizes the argument each sister makes and supports his analysis with details and direct quotations from the text. Notice how the concluding sentence of this paragraph—"For Antigone, the unfair rule of a vengeful but victorious leader may be rightfully broken so that the more important rules of family and faith can prevail"—concisely summarizes Antigone's position and ties directly to the writing prompt and the thesis statement made in the introduction. The student closes by returning, and dramatically, to Sophocles's purpose as he sees it: "Sophocles shows that Antigone, whatever her choice, will have to live, or die, with the consequences of her actions."

All three body paragraphs use **transition words** to show relationships between the main points within and between the body paragraphs. Words and phrases such as "**In the opening scene,**" "**immediately,**" "**initial**" and "**later**" signal sequential, or chronological, transitions. Other transitional words and phrases, such as "**however,**" "**to the contrary,**" and "**also,**" indicate that comparisons and contrasts are being used as transitions. In this context, a text-specific line such as "**To the animals' surprise**" is a transitional phrase as well, linking a democratic debate with an unexpected coup. Without transitions as a guide, connecting such different works as *Antigone* and *Animal Farm* would be difficult to follow.

## PRACTICE

Write one body paragraph for your literary analysis essay that follows the suggested format. When you are finished, trade with a partner and offer each other feedback. How effective is the topic sentence at stating the main point of the paragraph? How strong is the evidence used to support the topic sentence? Does the analysis thoroughly support the topic sentence? Is the analysis effectively organized, with strong transitions to connect and clarify ideas? Offer each other suggestions, and remember that they are most helpful when they are constructive.

# SKILL: CONCLUSIONS

## DEFINE

The conclusion is the final paragraph or section of a nonfiction text. In argumentative text, the conclusion brings the discussion to a close. It follows directly from the introduction and body of the text by referring back to the ideas presented there. A conclusion should restate the thesis statement and summarize the main ideas covered in the body of the text. Depending on the type of text, a conclusion might also include a recommendation or solution, a call to action, or a statement of insight. Many conclusions try to connect with readers by encouraging them to apply what they have learned from the text to their own lives.

## IDENTIFICATION AND APPLICATION

When writing conclusions for a literary analysis:

- Provide a concluding paragraph that follows from and supports the thesis statement presented in the introduction and developed in the body paragraphs.
- Reference key points, important supporting details, and the names of titles and authors discussed.
- Avoid including new information not previously mentioned or developed.
- Consider other options in addition to simply summarizing information previously presented, such as including a call to action or leaving readers with an interesting final thought.

## MODEL

An effective conclusion sums up the argument developed throughout the essay and leaves a lasting impression on the audience. In the conclusion of the Student Model, "Breaking the Rules," the writer returns to ideas established

in the introduction, summarizes the information that helped prove the thesis, and concludes with a restatement of the original thesis.

> ***In summary,*** *the main characters of both texts think they are right to overthrow what they see as unfair rules. That said, the breaking of rules may result in dire consequences. For Antigone, death may be the punishment she pays for disobeying Creon's edict. For the creatures living on Animal Farm, the breaking of the rules merely changes the leadership of the farm, but it does not improve the lives of the animals.* ***In short, rules may be justifiably broken, but not without unintended and often unpleasant consequences.***

The transition "In summary" lets the reader know that this is the concluding paragraph, although it is important to note that there are other ways to create stronger transitions. Since the author draws similarities between literature and life, which is a memorable and interesting way to conclude the analysis, another way of beginning the concluding paragraph might be, "As often happens with people even today." The conclusion effectively restates the thesis in its final line: "In short, rules may be justifiably broken, but not without unintended and often unpleasant consequences." It also briefly summarizes important details explored in the body of the analysis, such as the consequences the characters in both texts face as a result of their decisions to challenge the rules. While the writer used the body of the essay to delve deeply into such evidence drawn from the sources, the conclusion contains a short summary of what was proven.

## PRACTICE

Write a conclusion for your essay. Your essay should reinforce or restate your thesis, briefly summarize important ideas, and effectively wrap up your analysis. Exchange conclusions with a peer review partner when you are finished and offer each other feedback.

NOTES

# DRAFT

CA-CCSS: CA.RI.9-10.1, CA.RI.9-10.2, CA.W.9-10.1a, CA.W.9-10.1b, CA.W.9-10.1c, CA.W.9-10.1e, CA.W.9-10.4, CA.W.9-10.5, CA.W.9-10.6, CA.W.9-10.10, CA.SL.9-10.1a, CA.SL.9-10.1c, CA.SL.9-10.1d, CA.L.9-10.1b

## WRITING PROMPT

Rules have played an important role in societies around the world and across the ages. What the rules are, why they matter, how they are broken, and why some people feel they must break them are central concerns in many texts from this unit, which seeks to answer the essential question, *When is it appropriate to challenge the rules?* Write a literary analysis of two selections you have read during the unit, examining how the authors explore the issue of when it is appropriate to challenge the rules.

Your literary analysis should include:

- an introduction that
  - presents a reasonable claim, expressed in a clear thesis statement
  - names the author and title of each text you have selected to support your claim
- body paragraphs that
  - present a thorough analysis of your claim
  - contain textual evidence and details to support your claim
  - demonstrate a logical organization of ideas
- a conclusion paragraph that
  - restates your thesis statement
  - effectively wraps up your essay
  - leaves your reader with a lasting impression, perhaps through an interesting final thought

You have already made progress toward writing your own literary analysis. You have thought about your audience and purpose and examined the texts you have read in this unit to choose two you will address in your essay. You have created a thesis statement and analyzed the text evidence to choose details that will support the claim in that thesis statement. You have considered

how best to organize the information you have drawn from the texts into strong body paragraphs with main ideas and how to provide clear transitions to show the connections between ideas. You have drafted an introduction that states your claim and a conclusion that restates it in a unique way and leaves a lasting impression. Now it is time to write a draft of your literary analysis.

Use your essay road map and other prewriting materials to help you as you write. Remember that argumentative writing begins with an introduction and presents a claim in the form of a thesis statement. Body paragraphs develop the claim in the thesis statement with strong supporting reasons, details, quotations, and other relevant information from the texts. Transitions help the reader understand the relationship among the claim, supporting reasons, and evidence. A concluding paragraph summarizes or reflects on the information in the essay and restates the thesis statement to remind readers why the thesis statement is sound and correct.

When drafting, ask yourself these questions:

- What is the most important thing I want to say in this essay?
- How can I best present the claim in my thesis statement?
- What facts, details, and quotations can I draw from the texts to provide strong support for my claims?
- Have I taken the time to analyze each piece of evidence I have chosen?
- Am I remembering to relate all the evidence to my thesis statement?
- Does the evidence I've chosen represent a thorough understanding of the texts?
- How can I use precise language to present my claims and evidence in a way that is interesting to the reader?
- How well have I communicated each writer's portrayal of a situation in which it is appropriate to challenge the rules?
- What do I want my readers to believe or think once they have finished reading my essay?

Before you submit your draft, read it over carefully. You want to be sure that you have responded to all aspects of the prompt.

NOTES

# REVISE

**CA-CCSS:** CA.RI.9-10.1, CA.W.9-10.1a, CA.W.9-10.1b, CA.W.9-10.1c, CA.W.9-10.1d, CA.W.9-10.1e, CA.W.9-10.4, CA.W.9-10.5, CA.W.9-10.6, CA.W.9-10.10, CA.SL.9-10.1a, CA.SL.9-10.1c, CA.SL.9-10.1d, CA.L.9-10.1a, CA.L.9-10.1b, CA.L.9-10.2c

## WRITING PROMPT

Rules have played an important role in societies around the world and across the ages. What the rules are, why they matter, how they are broken, and why some people feel they must break them are central concerns in many texts from this unit, which seeks to answer the essential question, *When is it appropriate to challenge the rules?* Write a literary analysis of two selections you have read during the unit, examining how the authors explore the issue of when it is appropriate to challenge the rules.

Your literary analysis should include:

- an introduction that
  - presents a reasonable claim, expressed in a clear thesis statement
  - names the author and title of each text you have selected to support your claim
- body paragraphs that
  - present a thorough analysis of your claim
  - contain textual evidence and details to support your claim
  - demonstrate a logical organization of ideas
- a conclusion paragraph that
  - restates your thesis statement
  - effectively wraps up your essay
  - leaves your reader with a lasting impression, perhaps through an interesting final thought

You have written a draft of your literary analysis. You have also received input from your peers about how to improve it. Now you are going to revise your draft.

Here are some recommendations to help you revise:

- Review the suggestions made by your peers.
- Focus on maintaining a formal style. A formal style suits your purpose of making a claim about academic texts. It is also appropriate for an audience of peers, teachers, and other readers interested in learning more about the themes and messages of literary texts.
  - › As you revise, replace slang with formal diction.
  - › Remove any first-person pronouns such as "I," "me," or "mine" or instances of addressing readers as "you," as well as any contractions or other shorthand. This will help you maintain a formal, rather than conversational or personal, writing style.
  - › Remove any emotional or biased language from your writing that interferes with an objective tone.
  - › Find places where you have shifted verb tense, could combine short sentences and break up run-on sentences, or might otherwise adjust your writing to elevate its quality.
  - › Verify that your claims are supported by textual evidence and not personal opinion.
  - › Use active voice rather than passive voice whenever possible in supporting your claims.

- After you have revised elements of style, think about ways to improve your essay's content and organization.
  - › Is your claim stated clearly in your thesis statement?
  - › Does your introduction present your thesis statement and the texts you will discuss in your essay, as well as engage readers?
  - › Is your argument logically organized? What sections could be reorganized to clarify your ideas?
  - › Do your body paragraphs contain strong main points and clear transitions that smoothly link the ideas in your essay?
  - › Do the reasons and evidence in your body paragraphs support your thesis statement and main points?
  - › Do you need to add any new textual evidence to fully support the claim in your thesis statement?
  - › Have you evaluated the strengths and weaknesses of any of the evidence you used to support your claim? Did you remove or edit weak or less relevant evidence?
  - › Do your word choices make sense and engage the reader?
  - › Have you presented readers with a strong conclusion that also supports your thesis statement?

# SKILL: SOURCES AND CITATIONS

## DEFINE

Sources are the documents and information that authors use to develop their writing. A **primary source** is direct evidence from a specific time and place. It includes any material that was produced by eyewitnesses to an event or who lived during an historical period. In the case of an argumentative essay involving a literary analysis, the primary source is the original literary text being analyzed, such as the novel *Animal Farm*. **Secondary sources,** in contrast, interpret and analyze primary sources. These sources are one or more steps removed from an event. For example, an essay or article about the novel *Animal Farm* is a secondary source that a writer might consult when writing about the novel. **Citations** provide information within the text about the sources an author used to write a text or essay. Citations are required whenever authors quote someone else's words or refer to someone else's ideas in their writing. They let readers know who originally came up with these words and ideas. When writing a literary analysis, writers cannot simply make up information, or draw on their personal opinions or ideas. To make a convincing argument, writers must use solid research from reliable sources. If an author does not identify sources of information, the quality of the text will suffer and the writer may be accused of plagiarism.

## IDENTIFICATION AND APPLICATION

- Sources can be primary or secondary in nature. Primary sources are original creative works, first-hand accounts, artifacts, or other original materials. Examples of primary sources include:
  - Poems, plays, novels
  - Letters or other correspondence
  - Autobiographies or memoirs
  - Diaries, personal journals, or speeches
  - Photographs
  - Official documents

- › Eyewitness accounts and interviews
- › Audio recordings and radio broadcasts
- › Works of art
- › Artifacts

- Secondary sources interpret and analyze primary sources. Secondary sources are the written interpretation and analysis of primary source materials. Some examples of secondary sources include:
  - › Commentary or criticisms
  - › Encyclopedia articles
  - › Textbooks
  - › Histories
  - › Documentary films
  - › News analyses

- Whether sources are primary or secondary, they must be **credible** and **accurate.** Writers of informative/explanatory texts look for sources from experts in the topic they are writing about.
  - › When researching online, they look for URLs that contain ".gov" (government agencies), ".edu" (colleges and universities), and ".org" (museums and other non-profit organizations).
  - › Writers also use respected print and online news and information sources.

- Anytime a writer uses words from another source exactly as they are written, the words must appear in quotation marks. Quotation marks show that the words are not the author's own words but are borrowed from another source. In the Student Model essay, the writer uses quotation marks around words taken directly from the source *Antigone*:

  **"Go thine own way; myself will bury him, / How sweet to die in such employ, to rest— / Sister and brother linked in love's embrace— / A sinless sinner, banned awhile on earth, / But by the dead commended; and with them I shall abide for ever. As for thee, / Scorn if thou wilt, the eternal laws of Heaven" (Sophocles).**

- A writer includes a citation to give credit to any source, whether primary or secondary, that is quoted exactly. There are several different ways to cite a source. One way is to put the author's last name in parenthesis at the end of the sentence in which the quote appears. This is what the writer of the Student Model essay does after the quotation above. Notice that the punctuation goes after the second parenthesis.
- Citations are also necessary when a writer borrows ideas from another source, even if the writer paraphrases, or puts those ideas in his or her

own words. Citations demonstrate that the writer did credible work, but they also help readers discover where they can learn more.

## MODEL

In this excerpt from the Student Model essay, the writer includes quotations from George Orwell's novel *Animal Farm* as support for his main point.

> In his novel *Animal Farm,* George Orwell also deals with the importance of rules to social order. As in Antigone, the rules of Animal Farm seem to be justifiably broken, but for different reasons and with different consequences. After the animal's initial overthrow of Mr. Jones's rule, Snowball and Napoleon vie for leadership. A debate over the building of the windmill precedes what is supposed to be a democratic vote by all the animals. To the animals' surprise, the democratic rules of debate and voting are violated when the meeting turns into a military-style coup as Napoleon uses his trained dogs to viciously attack Snowball and chase him off the farm. Having seized power, Napoleon immediately changes the existing rules so he can maintain iron-fisted control. **"He [Napoleon] announced that from now on the Sunday-morning meetings would come to an end.... In future all questions relating to the working of the farm would be settled by a special committee of pigs, presided over by himself" (Orwell).** Later, Napoleon sends Squeaker around the farm to explain the new rules. **Squeaker tells the animals, "No one believes more firmly than Comrade Napoleon that all animals are equal. He would be only too happy to let you make your decisions for yourselves. But sometimes you might make the wrong decisions, comrades, and then where should we be?" (Orwell).** The animals had justifiably broken rules when they overthrew their human masters. Nonetheless, the animals are eventually subjected to the same type of autocratic control that they had sought to overthrow.

The writer announces the name of the text and the author of that text in the paragraph's opening. When quoting directly, the writer included the author's name in parentheses "(Orwell)" and placed a period after each citation. There are two kinds of quotations, though they are treated the same way: The first is by the narrator, and the other is a character's dialogue. To avoid an awkward quote-within-a-quote in the second quotation, the writer identifies the speaker, Squeaker, and then punctuates the dialogue in regular quotation marks. Notice, too, how the writer uses a bracketed note to clarify who "He"

NOTES

is in a long quotation: "[Napoleon]." This is used when a quotation makes reference to previous lines and includes, then, an ambiguous pronoun. All of this effort on the part of the writer makes the work of reading that much easier for the audience.

Now, note the way in which the student writer's in-text citation references information in the Works Cited page that follows the essay:

**Works Cited**

Orwell, George. *Animal Farm. StudySync.* BookheadEd Learning, LLC., 2015. Web. 19 July 2015.

Sophocles. *Antigone. StudySync.* BookheadEd Learning, LLC., 2015. Web. 19 July 2015.

The full Works Cited page provides complete bibliographic information for each source referenced in the essay. As both of the sources you will use for your essay come from the StudySync website, **follow these rules for citing information from a website on a Works Cited page:**

Last, First M. "Article or Page Title." *Website Title.* Website Publisher. Date Month Year Published (if available). Web. Date Month Year Accessed.

As a quick reference, follow the Student Model example when preparing your Works Cited page, adjusting author names and text titles as necessary. Note that book and play titles are italicized, while essay, speech, and poem titles appear in quotation marks.

## PRACTICE

Select a paragraph from your essay and double-check that you have cited your sources correctly. When you are finished, trade with a partner and offer each other feedback. How successful was the writer in citing sources for the essay? Offer each other suggestions, and remember that they are most helpful when they are constructive.

NOTES

# EDIT, PROOFREAD, AND PUBLISH

**CA-CCSS:** CA.RI.9-10.1, CA.W.9-10.1a, CA.W.9-10.1b, CA.W.9-10.1c, CA.W.9-10.1d, CA.W.9-10.1e, CA.W.9-10.4, CA.W.9-10.5, CA.W.9-10.6, CA.W.9-10.9a, CA.W.9-10.10, CA.SL.9-10.1a, CA.L.9-10.1a, CA.L.9-10.1b, CA.L.9-10.2a, CA.L.9-10.2b, CA.L.9-10.2c, CA.L.9-10.3a

## WRITING PROMPT

Rules have played an important role in societies around the world and across the ages. What the rules are, why they matter, how they are broken, and why some people feel they must break them are central concerns in many texts from this unit, which seeks to answer the essential question, *When is it appropriate to challenge the rules?* Write a literary analysis of two selections you have read during the unit, examining how the authors explore the issue of when it is appropriate to challenge the rules.

Your literary analysis should include:

- an introduction that
  - › presents a reasonable claim, expressed in a clear thesis statement
  - › names the author and title of each text you have selected to support your claim
- body paragraphs that
  - › present a thorough analysis of your claim
  - › contain textual evidence and details to support your claim
  - › demonstrate a logical organization of ideas
- a conclusion paragraph that
  - › restates your thesis statement
  - › effectively wraps up your essay
  - › leaves your reader with a lasting impression, perhaps through an interesting final thought

You have revised your literary analysis essay and received input from your peers on that revision. Now it's time to edit and proofread your essay to produce a final version. Here are some questions you asked yourself prior to this stage. Review this list once more to ensure that your essay is appropriate to the task and meets the requirements of a literary analysis:

- Is my introduction engaging, and does it effectively present my thesis statement?
- Have I included strong reasons and sound evidence to support the claim in my thesis statement?
- Have I accurately cited the sources from which I have drawn textual evidence, both within the body of my essay and in my Works Cited list?
- Does the evidence I have chosen represent the strongest and most relevant support for my claim?
- Have I organized my essay so that my body paragraphs each contain a clear main idea and supporting details?
- Have I used clear transitions to show the connections between ideas in my essay?
- Have I presented the reader with a conclusion that effectively wraps up my essay?
- Have I fully proven the validity of my claim to readers?
- Have I eliminated any examples of informal language or unobjective tone?
- Have I incorporated all the valuable suggestions from my peers?

When you are satisfied with your work, move on to proofread it for errors:

- Check that you have formatted your essay according to approved guidelines and standards. This includes title page or title placement, margins, font, spacing, paragraphing, bibliographic information, and other technical considerations.
- Check your spelling, including names of authors, titles, and characters.
- Check sentence structure, including use of compound sentences and parallel structure.
- Check punctuation. Look for missing or misplaced commas and confirm that you have used semicolons and colons correctly.
- Check that you have used italics correctly.
- Check the content and punctuation of quotations and citations.

Once you have made all your corrections, you are ready to submit and publish your work. You can distribute your writing to family and friends, hang it on a bulletin board, or post it on your blog. If you publish online, create links to your sources and citations, to help readers investigate your sources and learn more about the texts you have analyzed.

PHOTO/IMAGE CREDITS:

Cover, ©iStock.com/prudkov, ©iStock.com, ©iStock.com/alexey_boldin, ©iStock.com/skegbydave
p. iii, ©iStock.com/DNY59, ©iStock.com/alexey_boldin, ©iStockphoto.com, ©iStock.com/Massonstock
p. iv, ©iStockphoto.com/Urs Siedentop
p. vii, ©iStock.com/moevin, ©iStock.com/skegbydave, ©iStock.com/Chemlamp, ©iStock.com/svariophoto
p. 2, ©iStock.com/prudkov
p. 4, ©iStock.com/franckreporter
p. 9, ©iStock.com/jiduha
p. 13, ©iStock.com/tunart
p. 19, ©iStock.com/Allkindza
p. 25, ©iStock.com/MariaArefyeva
p. 30, ©iStock.com/narvikk
p. 36, ©iStock.com/traveler1116
p. 41, ©iStock.com/subman
p. 45, Henry Groskinsky/contributor/Getty Images
p. 52, ©iStock.com/DanBrandenburg
p. 59, ©iStock.com/fstockfoto
p. 65, ©iStock.com/valterdias
p. 72, ©iStock.com/EcoPic
p. 81, ©iStock.com/wundervisuals
p. 90, ©iStock.com/moevin, ©iStock.com/svariophoto
p. 91, ©iStock.com/moevin, ©iStock.com/skegbydave
p. 96, ©iStock.com/moevin, ©iStock.com/skegbydave
p. 98, ©iStock.com/Chemlamp, ©iStock.com/skegbydave
p. 100, ©iStock.com/THEPALMER, ©iStock.com/skegbydave
p. 105, ©iStock.com/shaunl, ©iStock.com/skegbydave
p. 109, ©iStock.com/moevin, ©iStock.com/skegbydave
p. 113, ©iStock.com/bo1982, ©iStock.com/skegbydave
p. 116, ©iStock.com/Jeff_Hu, ©iStock.com/skegbydave
p. 121, ©iStock.com/stevedangers, ©iStock.com/skegbydave
p. 123, ©iStock.com/moevin, ©iStock.com/skegbydave
p. 125, ©iStock.com/moevin, ©iStock.com/skegbydave
p. 127, ©iStock.com/mmac72, ©iStock.com/skegbydave
p. 131, ©iStock.com/moevin, ©iStock.com/skegbydave

# Text Fulfillment Through StudySync

If you are interested in specific titles, please fill out the form below and we will check availability through our partners.

## ORDER DETAILS

Date:

| TITLE | AUTHOR | Paperback/ Hardcover | Specific Edition *If Applicable* | Quantity |
|---|---|---|---|---|
| | | | | |
| | | | | |
| | | | | |
| | | | | |
| | | | | |
| | | | | |
| | | | | |
| | | | | |
| | | | | |
| | | | | |

### SHIPPING INFORMATION

Contact:
Title:
School/District:
Address Line 1:
Address Line 2:
Zip or Postal Code:
Phone:
Mobile:
Email:

### BILLING INFORMATION

☐ *SAME AS SHIPPING*

Contact:
Title:
School/District:
Address Line 1:
Address Line 2:
Zip or Postal Code:
Phone:
Mobile:
Email:

### PAYMENT INFORMATION

☐ CREDIT CARD

Name on Card:

Card Number: Expiration Date: Security Code:

☐ PO

Purchase Order Number:

StudySync Text Fulfillment, BookheadEd Learning, LLC
610 Daniel Young Drive | Sonoma, CA 95476